ACTIVE

SKILLS FOR READING 2

Neil J Anderson

NATIONAL GEOGRAPHIC LEARNING | HEINLE CENGAGE Learning

Australia • Brazil • Japan • Korea • Mexico • Singapore • Spain • United Kingdom • United States

NATIONAL GEOGRAPHIC LEARNING | HEINLE CENGAGE Learning·

Active Skills for Reading Student Book 2, Third Edition

Neil J Anderson

Publisher, Asia and Global ELT:
Andrew Robinson

Senior Development Editor: Derek Mackrell

Associate Development Editor: Sarah Tan

Director of Global Marketing: Ian Martin

Academic Marketing Manager: Emily Stewart

Marketing Communications Manager:
Beth Leonard

Director of Content and Media Production:
Michael Burggren

Associate Content Project Manager:
Mark Rzeszutek

Manufacturing Manager: Marcia Locke

Manufacturing Planner:
Mary Beth Hennebury

Composition: PreMediaGlobal

Cover Design: Page2, LLC

Freelance writer: John Murn

Freelance editor: Jenny Wilsen

For product information and technology assistance, contact us at
Cengage Learning Customer & Sales Support, 1-800-354-9706

For permission to use material from this text or product, submit all requests online at **cengage.com/permissions**
Further permissions questions can be emailed to
permissionrequest@cengage.com

ISBN-13: 978-1-133-30803-4
ISBN-10: 1-133-30803-1

National Geographic Learning
20 Channel Center Street
Boston, MA 02210
USA

Cengage Learning is a leading provider of customized learning solutions with office locations around the globe, including Singapore, the United Kingdom, Australia, Mexico, Brazil, and Japan. Locate your local office at:
international.cengage.com/region

Cengage Learning products are represented in Canada by Nelson Education, Ltd.

Visit Heinle online at **elt.heinle.com**
Visit our corporate website at **www.cengage.com**

Photo credits

FRONT MATTER: Thinkstock: Hemera/Getty Images, Jupiterimages/Getty Images, Jupiterimages/Getty Images, Hemera/Getty Images. **p11:** iStockphoto/Thinkstock (tr), Wavebreak Media/Thinkstock (tl), Ryan McVay/Photodisc/Thinkstock (br), iStockphoto/Thinkstock (bl). **p13:** Hemera/Thinkstock. **p17:** iStockphoto/Thinkstock. **p20:** Jupiterimages/Getty Images/Comstock/Thinkstock. **p21:** iStockphoto/Thinkstock (tr), Stockbyte/Thinkstock (br), Medioimages/Photodisc/Thinkstock (tl), altrendo images/Stockbyte/Thinkstock (bl). **p23:** © Cengage Learning 2014 (cr), Brand X Pictures/Thinkstock (t), iStockphoto/Thinkstock (cr), iStockphoto/Thinkstock (br), iStockphoto/Thinkstock (br). **p25:** Hemera/Thinkstock. **p27:** Stockbyte/Thinkstock (tr), Jupiterimages/Goodshoot/Thinkstock (cl). **p31:** Felicia Martinez/PhotoEdit. **p33:** GYI NSEA/iStockphoto.Com (tc), AF archive/Alamy (tr), AF archive/Alamy (cl), AF archive/Alamy (tl). **p36:** Archives du 7eme Art/Photos 12/Alamy (tc), AF archive/Alamy (tr), Archives du 7e Art/Photos 12/Alamy (tc). **p37:** Mathew Imaging/FilmMagic/Getty Images. **p45:** Rune Hellestad/Corbis (t), AF archive/Alamy (b). **p47:** EVERETT KENNEDY BROWN/EPA/Newscom. **p49:** Comstock/Thinkstock Images/Thinkstock (tl), Comstock/Jupiterimages/Getty Images/Thinkstock (bl), Jupiterimages/Getty Images/Thinkstock (tr), iStockphoto/Thinkstock (br). **p51:** MICHAEL KOOREN/Reuters/Landov. **p54:** lev radin/Shutterstock .com (tl), ZUMA Wire Service/Alamy Limited (tc), s_bukley / Shutterstock.com (tr). **p55:** Mai Techaphan/Shutterstock.com. **p59:** Arcady/Shutterstock.com (tc), ancroft/Shutterstock.com (cl), 3drenderings/Shutterstock.com (cr). **p61:** iStockphoto/Thinkstock. **p64:** Hugh Lansdown/Shutterstock.com (tc), VStock/Thinkstock (tc), Micha Klootwijk/Shutterstock.com (tl), iStockphoto/Thinkstock (tr). **p65:** Sacramento Bee/Getty Images. **p71:** iStockphoto/Thinkstock (tr), Jupiterimages/Comstock/Thinkstock (bl). **p75:** iStockphoto/Thinkstock. **p83:** lev radin/Shutterstock.com. **p85:** Tom Briglia/FilmMagic/Getty Images. **p87:** iStockphoto/Thinkstock. (tr), Digital Vision/Thinkstock (tl). **p89:** Luis Marden/National Geographic Image Collection. **p97:** Everett Collection/Shutterstock.com (tl), Library of Congress Prints and Photographs Division(LC-DIG-hec-29043) (cr), Library of Congress Prints & Photographs Division (LC-USF34-045666-D) (cl). **p99:** leedsn/Shutterstock.com (cr). **p102:** Jupiterimages/Polka Dot/Thinkstock (tl), iStockphoto/Thinkstock (tr), Digital Vision/Thinkstock (cl). **p103:** Comstock/Thinkstock (cr), Digital Vision/Thinkstock (bl), Jupiterimages/Comstock/Thinkstock (tl). **p107:** Comstock/Thinkstock (tl), iStockphoto/Thinkstock (tr), iStockphoto/Thinkstock (cl), iStockphoto/Thinkstock (cr). **p109:** Photos.com/Thinkstock (cl), iStockphoto/Thinkstock (tr). **p113:** Ingram Publishing/Thinkstock (t), © 2011 GREG DALE/National Geographic Image Collection (cr). **p118:** HANDOUT/MCT/Newscom. **p121:** iStockphoto/Thinkstock (tr), Comstock/Thinkstock (br). **p123:** iStockphoto/Thinkstock (tr), iStockphoto/Thinkstock (cl). **p125:** DeepGreen/Shutterstock.com (t), Alan Copson/Getty Images (cl), Jeff Morgan 02/Alamy (cr). **p126:** AP Photo/Frank Franklin II (tl), INTERFOTO/Alamy (tr). **p127:** Tony Bowler/Shutterstock.com (cr), Comstock/Thinkstock (t). **p130:** iStockphoto/Thinkstock (tl), iStockphoto/Thinkstock (tr). **p131:** eyewave/iStockphoto.com (cl), Kosarev Alexander/Shutterstock.com (br). **p136:** iStockphoto/Thinkstock (tl), Stockbyte/Ciaran Griffin/Thinkstock (tr), iStockphoto/Thinkstock (cl), iStockphoto/Thinkstock (cr). **p137:** iStockphoto/Thinkstock (tr), branislavpudar/Shutterstock.com (cl), iStockphoto/Thinkstock (tr), iStockphoto/Thinkstock (cl), Adisa/Shutterstock.com (cr). **p141:** iStockphoto/Thinkstock (tl), madebyanton/Shutterstock.com (tl), Christoph Weihs/Shutterstock.com (tr). **p145:** madebyanton/Shutterstock.com (tl), Christoph Weihs/Shutterstock.com (tr). **p147:** Patrick Riviere/Getty Images (tr), AP Photo/Andy Wong (cr). **p159:** iStockphoto/Thinkstock. **p161:** Quickimage RM/Glow Images, Inc. (cr), © AMY TOENSING/National Geographic Image Collection (cl). **p156:** © TODD GIPSTEIN/National Geographic Image Collection.

Printed in China
5 6 7 16 15 14

Dedication & Acknowledgments

This book is dedicated to the students and teachers who have used *ACTIVE Skills for Reading* over the past ten years. Since 2002/2003 when the first edition of *ACTIVE Skills for Reading* was published, thousands of students and teachers have used the book. I know that I had no idea that the series would be this popular and that we would reach the stage of publishing a third edition.

The pedagogical framework for this series is as viable today as it has ever been. As students and teachers use each of the elements of *ACTIVE*, stronger reading will result.

My associations with the editorial team in Singapore continue to be some of my greatest professional relationships. I express appreciation to Sean Bermingham, Derek Mackrell, Andrew Robinson, and Sarah Tan for their commitment to excellence in publishing. I also express appreciation to Jenny Wilsen and John Murn for their commitment to helping the third edition be stronger than the two previous editions.

Neil J Anderson

The third edition of *ACTIVE Skills For Reading* maintains the ACTIVE approach developed by reading specialist Professor Neil J Anderson, while introducing several significant improvements.

This new edition now has a full color design, presenting the series' content in an attractive and student-friendly way. Approximately half of the passages have been replaced with new and engaging topics; the rest have been updated. It also has a wide variety of text types including articles, journals, blogs, and interviews, with later levels featuring readings based on content from National Geographic.

Each of the 24 chapters now includes a "Motivational Tips" section from Professor Anderson, reflecting his current research into student motivation and learning. His reading charts have also been updated to more accurately track students' reading fluency and comprehension progress.

ACTIVE Skills for Reading, Third Edition features an Assessment CD-ROM with ExamView® Pro, which has been revised to reflect the needs of learners preparing for standardized tests.

This latest edition of *ACTIVE Skills for Reading* series is designed to further enhance students' progress, helping them to become more confident, independent, and ACTIVE readers.

Reviewers for this edition

Mardelle Azimi; **Jose Carmona** Hillsborough Community College; **Grace Chao** Soochow University; **Mei-Rong Alice Chen** National Taiwan University of Science and Technology; **Irene Dryden; Jennifer Farnell** Greenwich Japanese School; **Kathy Flynn** Glendale Community College; **Sandy Hartmann** University of Houston; **Joselle L. LaGuerre; Margaret V. Layton; Myra M. Medina** Miami Dade College; **Masumi Narita** Tokyo International University; **Margaret Shippey** Miami Dade College; **Satoshi Shiraki; Karen Shock** Savannah College of Art and Design; **Sandrine Ting; Colin S. Ward** Lonestar College; **Virginia West** Texas A&M University; **James B. Wilson; Ming-Nuan Yang** Chang Gung Institute of Technology; **Jakchai Yimngam** Rajamangala University of Technology

Reviewers of the second edition

Chiou-lan Chern National Taiwan Normal University; **Cheongsook Chin** English Campus Institute, Inje University; **Yang Hyun** Jung-Ang Girls' High School; **Li Junhe** Beijing No.4 High School; **Tim Knight** Gakushuin Women's College; **Ahmed M. Motala** University of Sharjah; **Gleides Ander Nonato** Colégio Arnaldo and Centro Universitário Newton Paiva; **Ethel Ogane** Tamagawa University; **Seung Ku Park** Sunmoon University; **Shu-chien, Sophia, Pan** College of Liberal Education, Shu-Te University; **Marlene Tavares de Almeida** Wordshop Escola de Linguas; **Naowarat Tongkam** Silpakorn University; **Nobuo Tsuda** Konan University; **Hasan Hüseyin Zeyrek** Istanbul Kültür University Faculty of Economics and Administrative Sciences

Contents

Vocabulary Learning Tips

Learning new vocabulary is an important part of learning to be a good reader. Remember that the letter **C** in **ACTIVE Skills for Reading** reminds us to **cultivate** vocabulary.

1 Decide if the word is worth learning now

As you read, you will find many words you do not know. You will slow your reading fluency if you stop at every new word. For example, you should stop to find out the meaning of a new word if:

    a. you read the same word many times.

    b. the word appears in the heading of a passage, or in the topic sentence of a paragraph—the sentence that gives the main idea of the paragraph.

2 Record information about new words you decide to learn

Keep a vocabulary notebook in which you write words you want to remember. Complete the following information for words that you think are important to learn:

New word	healthy
Translation	健康
Part of speech	adjective
Sentence where found	Oliver is well-known for sharing his secrets of cooking healthy food.
My own sentence	I exercise to stay fit and healthy.

3 Learn words from the same family

For many important words in English that you will want to learn, the word is part of a word family. As you learn new words, learn words in the family from other parts of speech (nouns, verbs, adjectives, adverbs, etc.).

Noun	happiness
Verb	
Adjective	happy
Adverb	happily

4 Learn words that go with the key word you are learning

When we learn new words, it is important to learn what other words are frequently used with them. These are called collocations. Here is an example from a student's notebook.

		long		
take		two-week		next week
go on	a	short	vacation	in Italy
need		summer		with my family
have		school		by myself

5 Create a word web

A word web is a picture that helps you connect words together and helps you increase your vocabulary. Here is a word web for the word *frightened*:

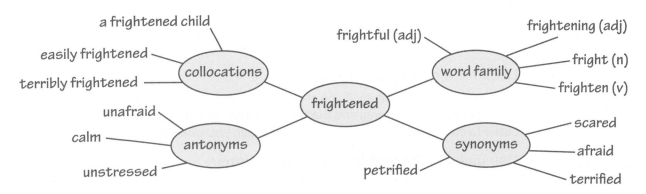

6 Memorize common prefixes, roots, and suffixes

Many English words can be divided into different parts. We call these parts *prefixes*, *roots*, and *suffixes*. A *prefix* comes at the beginning of a word, a *suffix* comes at the end of a word, and the *root* is the main part of the word. In your vocabulary notebook, make a list of prefixes and suffixes as you come across them. On page 175 there is a list of prefixes and suffixes in this book. For example, look at the word *unhappily*.

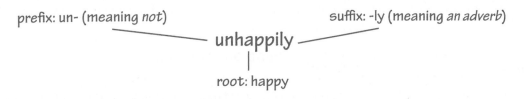

7 Regularly review your vocabulary notebook

You should review the words in your vocabulary notebook very often. The more often you review your list of new words, the sooner you will be able to recognize the words when you see them during reading. Set up a schedule to go over the words you are learning.

8 Make vocabulary flash cards

Flash cards are easy to make, and you can carry them everywhere with you. You can use them to study while you are waiting for the bus, walking to school or work, or eating a meal. You can use the flash cards with your friends to quiz each other. Here is an example of a flash card:

Front   Back

Tips for Fluent Reading

Find time to read every day.

Find the best time of day for you to read. Try to read when you are not tired. By reading every day, even for a short period, you will become a more fluent reader.

Look for a good place to read.

It is easier to read and study if you are comfortable. Make sure that there is good lighting in your reading area and that you are sitting in a comfortable chair. To make it easier to concentrate, try to read in a place where you won't be interrupted.

Use clues in the text to make predictions.

Fluent readers make predictions before and as they read. Use the title, subtitle, pictures, and captions to ask yourself questions about what you are going to read. Find answers to the questions when you read. After reading, think about what you have learned and decide what you need to read next to continue learning.

Establish goals before you read.

Before you read a text, think about the purpose of your reading. For example, do you just want to get a general idea of the passage? Or do you need to find specific information? Thinking about what you want to get from the reading will help you decide what reading skills you need to use.

Notice how your eyes and head are moving.

Good readers use their eyes, and not their heads, when they read. Moving your head back and forth when reading will make you tired. Practice avoiding head movements by placing your elbows on the table and resting your head in your hands. Do you feel movement as you read? If you do, hold your head still as you read. Also, try not to move your eyes back over a text. You should reread part of a text only when you have a specific purpose for rereading, for example, to make a connection between what you read previously and what you are reading now.

Try not to translate.

Translation slows down your reading. Instead of translating new words into your first language, first try to guess the meaning. Use the context (the other words around the new word) and word parts (prefixes, suffixes, and word roots) to help you guess the meaning.

Read in phrases rather than word by word.

Don't point at each word while you read. Practice reading in phrases—groups of words that go together.

Engage your imagination.

Good readers visualize what they are reading. They create a movie in their head of the story they are reading. As you read, try sharing with a partner the kinds of pictures that you create in your mind.

Avoid subvocalization.

Subvocalization means quietly saying the words as you read. You might be whispering the words or just silently saying them in your mind. Your eyes and brain can read much faster than you can speak. If you subvocalize, you can only read as fast as you can say the words. As you read, place your finger on your lips or your throat. Do you feel movement? If so, you are subvocalizing. Practice reading without moving your lips.

Don't worry about understanding every word.

Sometimes, as readers, we think we must understand the meaning of everything that we read. It isn't always necessary to understand every word in a passage in order to understand the meaning of the passage as a whole. Instead of interrupting your reading to find the meaning of a new word, circle the word and come back to it after you have finished reading.

Enjoy your reading.

Your enjoyment of reading will develop over time. Perhaps today you do not like to read in English, but as you read more, you should see a change in your attitude. The more you read in English, the easier it will become. You will find yourself looking forward to reading.

Read as much as you can.

The best tip to follow to become a more fluent reader is to read whenever and wherever you can. Good readers read a lot. They read many different kinds of material: newspapers, magazines, textbooks, websites, and graded readers. To practice this, keep a reading journal. Every day, make a list of the kinds of things you read during the day and how long you read each for. If you want to become a more fluent reader, read more!

Are You an ACTIVE Reader?

Before you use this book to develop your reading skills, think about your reading habits, and your strengths and weaknesses when reading in English. Check the statements that are true for you.

		Start of course	End of course
1	I read something in English every day.	☐	☐
2	I try to read where I'm comfortable and won't be interrupted.	☐	☐
3	I make predictions about what I'm going to read before I start reading.	☐	☐
4	I think about my purpose of reading before I start reading.	☐	☐
5	I keep my head still, and move only my eyes, when I read.	☐	☐
6	I try not to translate words from English to my first language.	☐	☐
7	I read in phrases rather than word by word.	☐	☐
8	I try to picture in my mind what I'm reading.	☐	☐
9	I read silently, without moving my lips.	☐	☐
10	I try to understand the meaning of the passage, and try not to worry about understanding the meaning of every word.	☐	☐
11	I usually enjoy reading in English.	☐	☐
12	I try to read as much as I can, especially outside class.	☐	☐

Follow the tips on pages 8–9. These will help you become a more active reader. At the end of the course, answer this quiz again to see if you have become a more fluent, active reader.

Exam Time

Getting Ready

Discuss the following questions with a partner.

1 How often do students take tests in your country? What kinds of tests do they take?

2 What kinds of tests do adults take? Which of these tests have you taken?

3 Are you good at taking tests? How do you prepare for them?

CHAPTER 1 For Better Grades—
Use Your Brain!

Before You Read
Do you remember?

A Think about answers to the following questions.

   1 Do you think you have a good memory? Why, or why not?

   2 What do you do when you need to remember something important?

   3 How do you usually study for a test?

B Discuss your answers with a partner.

Reading Skill
Describing a Process

> Some articles tell us how to do something. You can draw a diagram to help you understand things that are in a certain order. First, find the steps. Then, decide how best to arrange the steps in a diagram.

A Read the third paragraph of the article on the next page. Write the three kinds of memory described.

   1 _____

   2 _____

   3 _____

B Decide which diagram below is best for organizing the information above. Explain your answer to a partner.

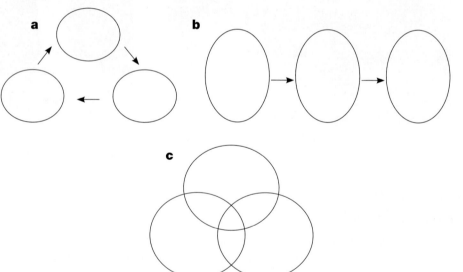

C Read the entire passage carefully. Then answer the questions on page 14.

> **Motivational Tip: I love reading—do you?** When I remember how much I like to read, it helps me stay positive, even when I have to read things that are not of my choice (like a textbook). Reading becomes much easier when you have a positive attitude.

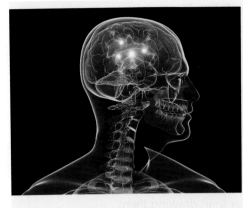

For Better Grades—Use Your Brain!

1 If you're like most students, you probably started this new **academic** year with a resolution to study harder. Now, science can help you keep your resolution. Recent discoveries in brain research point to better ways to learn.

2 How does the brain save new information? Think of the last time someone told you their phone
5 number. Could you remember that number five minutes later? Probably not! That's because it was in your short-term memory.

3 Our memory actually has three **components**. *Sensory memory* takes in information from our five senses and is stored for just a few seconds while our brain processes it. *Short-term memory* works like a "holding area" for new information—that's where you keep the phone number while you dial
10 it. But if you can put the phone number into *long-term memory*, you'll remember that same phone number next week. This part of your memory holds everything from irregular verbs to the names of all your cousins.

4 When you study, you **transfer** new information into **long-term** memory. Every time we learn something new, the **structure** of the brain actually changes as we build new connections to information that we
15 already know. When there are more connections to the new information, it's easier to find it again.

5 Brain researchers have discovered four key points for **effective** study.

1 **Make an effort.** The brain remembers better when we are interested in the subject, already know a little about it, and know we will need the information in the future.

2 Find the most important information and organize it. Your brain can process only a limited
20 amount of information at one time, so don't try to remember every detail. When studying a textbook, look for titles, headings, and illustrations to show you the main ideas.

3 Make the new brain connections stronger. One **technique** is to recite[1] the ideas out loud in your own words. This is the most powerful way to transfer information from short-term to long-term memory. Another method is drawing a picture of the information to activate the visual part of the brain.

25 **4** Give the new material time to soak in—your brain has to build new physical connections. For this reason, it's better to study for several short sessions than one long one. And cramming[2] the night before a big test doesn't help.

By understanding how the brain works, and following these four tips, you can make this your most successful academic year ever.

---

[1] When you **recite** something, you say it aloud after practicing or memorizing it.
[2] When you **cram** for an exam, you try to study for it in a short period of time.

Reading Comprehension
Check Your Understanding

A Choose the correct answers for the following questions.

1 Which topic is NOT discussed in the passage?
   a short and long-term memory
   b how to study for tests better
   c why some people are very smart

2 According to the passage, what does drawing a picture do?
   a It puts information into short-term memory.
   b It shows people you are trying to learn.
   c It makes the connections in the brain stronger.

3 Which sentence is most likely to be true?
   a Reciting ideas out loud is better than drawing them.
   b Brain researchers understand short-term memory best.
   c It's better to have information in your long-term memory when doing a test.

B Read the following sentences. Check (✔) true (T) or false (F).

		T	F
1	When we learn new facts, we save them in our long-term memory.		
2	You remember better if you start studying a long time before a test.		
3	Our brains change physically when we learn new information.		
4	Saying new information out loud is a good way to remember it.		
5	You don't have to memorize every small detail to learn a subject.		

Critical Thinking

C Discuss the following questions with a partner.

1 Which study techniques sound useful and which do not? Why? Have you tried any of them?

2 What other ideas do you have for how to study better?

Vocabulary Comprehension
Words in Context

A Choose the best answer. The words in blue are from the passage.

1 Some components of a healthy life are _____.
   a exercise and a good diet   b more energy and better skin

2 Which of these are long-term plans?
   a having a family   b going on holiday

3 You can transfer money _____.
   a at the bank   b in your wallet

4 You need to make an effort if a task is _____.

   a easy   **b** difficult

5 If you use effective ways to study, your grades will get _____.

   a better   **b** worse

6 The structure of something is how it is _____.

   a used   **b** organized

7 One technique for remembering new English words is _____.

   a writing them in a notebook   **b** taking an exam

8 Which of these is an academic skill?

   a writing an essay   **b** baking a cake

B **Answer the following questions, then discuss your answers with a partner. The words in blue are from the passage.**

   1 What are the main components of a computer?

   2 What is a useful technique for taking good notes in class?

   3 What do you think is the most effective way to manage stress?

   4 What are your long-term goals when it comes to learning English?

A **Look at the word web below. Are there other words you can think of to add to this web? Explain your diagram to a partner. How do your ideas connect to each other?**

Vocabulary Skill
Word Webs

> One helpful strategy that you can use to memorize new vocabulary is to create a *word web*. Word webs can help you remember the meaning of new vocabulary and relate this vocabulary to other words you know.

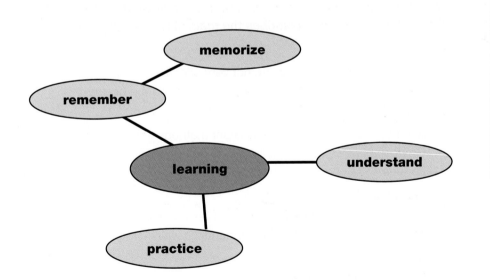

B **On a sheet of paper, create a word web using one of the categories in the box below (or one of your own). See how many branches and words you can add. Share your ideas with a partner.**

   travel   music   the future   food

CHAPTER 2 Oh, No! Not Another Test!

Before You Read
Too many tests?

A **Think about answers to the following questions.**

- a spoken English test
- a driving test
- a vocabulary quiz
- a test to get a job
- a piano or violin exam

- a school or university entrance exam
- a large international test like TOEFL® or IELTS®

1 Which of the tests above have you taken? Which ones are you planning to take?
2 Which do you find the most difficult? Why?
3 Which are the most important for your future?

B **Discuss your answers with a partner.**

Reading Skill
Identifying Main and Supporting Ideas

Every paragraph has a main idea, or topic. Often, you will find the main idea is given in the first or second sentence of a paragraph. Supporting ideas usually follow the main idea. Sentences with supporting ideas explain or give more information about the main idea.

A **Read paragraph 1 of the passage on the next page. Underline the sentence that best describes the main idea. Circle at least one supporting idea in the paragraph. Discuss your answers with a partner.**

B **Skim the rest of the passage, then read the following sentences. Circle the sentence that best describes the main idea of each paragraph.**

Paragraph 2
a Multiple-choice style tests are not very effective.
b Tests are easy to grade but the scores might not be useful.

Paragraph 3
a Reformers say that other assessment methods are better than tests.
b Group interviews and portfolios are two ways to assess a person's abilities.

Paragraph 4
a Some schools do not focus on giving tests to their students.
b Students can learn from other students as well their teachers.

Paragraph 5
a New test methods will continue to develop.
b There is no one best way to test learners.

C **Read the entire passage carefully. Then answer the questions on page 18.**

Oh, No! Not Another Test!

1 Think about the last test you took. How much of what you learned for the test do you still remember? Many people take tests to pass a course or get a promotion, but they often forget the information
5 afterward! This is especially the case for people taking large international tests like TOEFL or IELTS. These tests usually involve multiple-choice questions, and people often study to increase their scores, not to learn important information. In fact, educators are divided on whether these kinds of tests are the most effective way to **assess** a person's abilities.

2 Those who support such tests say they are the only way for educators and employers to
10 compare people based on their test scores. However, there are people trying to **reform** this system. They believe that standard tests aren't the best way to **measure** a person's ability. These reformers also believe that intelligent people are not always good at taking tests or **memorizing** facts. A multiple-choice test cannot always tell what people have learned, or whether they can **apply** that knowledge in the future.

3 15 Reformers believe that other types of evaluation achieve better results. Tests that contain a mix of written and spoken questions give a more complete assessment of what the person is capable of. A portfolio, or a collection of work done throughout a course, can show how much the student has improved individually. Group interviews, where a group of people are interviewed at the same time, can also be useful for employers, since they show how people
20 **interact** with others.

4 **Alternative** educational institutions, such as Montessori and Waldorf schools, don't believe that education should be focused on testing. At these schools, the classroom is very relaxed and "free," with students learning from each other as much as they learn from teachers. Some of these schools even allow students to choose what they study. Teachers
25 create activities designed to let students show their abilities or knowledge of a certain subject. In these schools, the focus is on learning by experiencing and doing things.

5 The **debate** on testing continues, and educators have yet to find a perfect method of evaluating learning. Until that day comes, old test methods will be used and new test methods will continue to be developed. But one thing's for sure, testing will continue to
30 play an important part in all our lives—so study hard!

Reading Comprehension
Check Your Understanding

A Match the sentence parts to make correct statements.

1 _____ Multiple-choice tests
2 _____ Portfolios
3 _____ Assessments
4 _____ Educational reformers
5 _____ Group interviews

a want to find better ways to evaluate students' abilities.
b let people demonstrate how they interact with others.
c have scores that are easy to compare.
d are examples of a student's work.
e are tests that measure how much a person has learned.

B Read the following sentences. Who would agree with each sentence? Check (✔) supporters *(S)* or reformers *(R)*.

		S	R
1	Multiple-choice tests are a good way to evaluate intelligence.		
2	It is important to see how students communicate with other people.		
3	Students learn better by experiencing instead of memorizing.		
4	A good test should allow examiners to easily compare people.		
5	The classroom should be a place where students prepare for tests.		

Critical Thinking

C Discuss the following questions with a partner.

1 Can you think of other alternatives to tests like TOEFL or IELTS?
2 Why do you think it is so hard to replace such tests with alternatives?

Vocabulary Comprehension
Definitions

A Match each word with its definition. The words in blue are from the passage.

1 _____ apply
2 _____ reform
3 _____ measure
4 _____ memorize
5 _____ assess
6 _____ interact
7 _____ alternative
8 _____ debate

a discussion about opinions on a topic
b to judge or evaluate someone or something
c to talk to each other or work together
d different than what is usual or expected
e to determine the size or amount of something
f to change or improve something
g remember something
h to use an idea or skill for a particular situation

B Complete the following sentences with the words in blue from **A**. You might have to change the form of the words.

1 You can tell she'll be a good mother from the way she _____ with children.
2 In a school _____, two teams will discuss the benefits and issues of a certain topic.
3 The new principal was considered a(n) _____. His main goal was to change the school's testing system and make it better.
4 The only way to learn irregular verb forms is to _____ them.

A Look at the following words and use the suffix *-ize* to write the verb form next to each one. Use your dictionary to help you with spelling.

1 standard _____
2 theory _____
3 modern _____
4 revolution _____
5 fantasy _____

Vocabulary Skill
The Suffix *-ize*

In this chapter you read the verb *memorize*. One common suffix in English is *-ize* (spelled *-ise* in British English), which means *to make* or *cause to become*.

B Match each verb above to its definition below.

1 _____: to form an idea or explanation about something
2 _____: to imagine or dream of having things you desire
3 _____: to change the way of doing something completely
4 _____: to bring something up-to-date; to make it current
5 _____: to make things the same or to fit a certain measurement

C Complete the following questions with a verb from **A**. Make sure you use the correct verb tense. Then answer the questions with a partner.

1 What would you do to _____ the look of your apartment?
2 Do you ever _____ about where you will live in the future?
3 Do you think the Internet has _____ the way people learn?

Motivational Tip: Using vocabulary skills. The vocabulary skills throughout this book can increase your range of vocabulary and help you with your general reading. How can you apply these vocabulary skills in your reading outside of class?

Real Life Skill
Reading Test Instructions

In an exam, understanding the test instructions, as well as the question itself, can help you to improve your test scores. Pay special attention to the verbs in the instructions, such as *choose, circle, underline, cross out, write,* or *explain.*

A **Below are four common types of questions used in tests. Read the instructions for each item. Then answer each question.**

1 Choose the word or phrase that best completes the sentence.

Mary is (a nice / the nicer / the nicest) person I have ever met.

2 Circle the sentence that best describes the photo.

a The man is looking for his key.
b The man is watching television.
c The man is getting dressed.
d The man is putting clothes in a suitcase.

3 Look at the word *one* in the sentence below. Underline the word or phrase that means the same as *one*.

I don't have a car now, but I want to buy one next year.

4 Write a sentence to describe the main idea of the passage below.

When should a person begin learning a second language? Is learning a second language not spoken in the home really easier for children? While many people think children are able to learn new languages easily, many experts now believe that second language learning can be as difficult for many children as it is for adults.

_____

_____

B **Discuss the following questions with a partner.**

1 What do you think each question type above is testing?
2 Which instructions were easiest to understand? Why?
3 Which question is easiest to give a score to? Which question is hardest?

What do you think?

1 What effect do tests have on education in your country?
2 Why do you think we need to take so many tests in modern society?
3 How you would design the perfect test? What kinds of questions would it have?

Going Abroad

Getting Ready

Discuss the following questions with a partner.
1 What do you like to do on vacation? Relax on a beach? Go shopping in a city?
2 Look at the photos above. Where are you able to do these activities?
3 Which of the places above would you most want to visit? Why?

CHAPTER 1 We're in Vietnam!

Before You Read
Travel Knowledge

A Answer the following questions.

1 What do you know about Vietnam? Write a few words about each topic.
   a location _____
   b climate _____
   c cities _____
   d history _____

2 Vietnam is becoming a very popular destination for tourists. Can you think of any reasons for this?

B Discuss your answers with a partner.

Reading Skill
Scanning for Details

An important use for scanning is to find a piece of information that we need. We do this in everyday life when we look up a word in the dictionary, or check a telephone number in the phone directory. Use scanning when you need to find a fact in a reading.

A Scan the passage on the next page and find the dates of the four blog posts.

Post 1: _____
Post 2: _____
Post 3: _____
Post 4: _____

B Read each blog post quickly to find the following information.

Post 1: Which city did they go to first? _____
Post 2: Where is the market that they visited? _____
Post 3: How long did they go hiking for? _____
Post 4: What is in Vung Tau? _____

C Now read the entire passage carefully. Then answer the questions on page 24.

Motivational Tip: Expect success! As you begin this chapter, what success do you expect to achieve? Do you expect to increase your reading fluency? Do you expect to increase your vocabulary? Success comes when you identify what you want to achieve and then work hard to achieve it. I challenge you to set a reasonable goal and expect success.

We're in Vietnam!

Posted on April 6 by Juliana

4

Hue is a **unique** city with lots to see. I would love to stay longer, but Tom and I are both ready for the beach. Tomorrow we'll take the train back to the south, and then we're going to a town called Vung Tau. It has several
5   beaches and is famous for crafts made out of seashells. Vietnam is an amazing country with so much variety—big modern cities, small traditional towns, mountains, jungles, and beaches. Two weeks here just isn't enough.

Posted on April 4 by Juliana

3

Now we're in the old capital city of Hue. After hiking around the Sapa mountains,
10   it's nice to have **accommodation** with electricity and a shower! Our trip to Sapa was long and **exhausting.** From there, we took a van to a small village in the mountains and went hiking for three days. The people who live there are called Hmong. They live a very **basic** life—no electricity or telephones. They don't have many **possessions,** but they are the kindest, friendliest people
15   I've ever met. Everyone smiles and says "hello." Tom and I can only speak a few words of Vietnamese, so smiling is the best way of communicating. This afternoon, we're taking a walking tour in Hue. We're going to visit the Forbidden Purple City, where the emperor lived.

Pagoda

Posted on March 27 by Juliana

2

20   Ho Chi Minh City is fantastic! The pagodas are **fabulous** and the different Buddha statues are wonderful to look at. We visited a market in Cholon, in the western part of the city, and saw an amazing **range** of fruits and vegetables. Everything was so colorful. We took hundreds of photographs! Later today we take the train north. We'll stay in Hanoi for two days, then catch a bus to Sapa.
25   Tom can't wait to go trekking in the mountains.

spring rolls

Posted on March 24 by Juliana

1

Greetings from Vietnam! Tom and I arrived here this afternoon tired but excited. This is our first trip to Asia and the friendliness of the people is amazing. All the different sights and smells make us **eager** to try everything—especially the
30   food! We're looking forward to eating spring rolls and pho for dinner. Our hotel is cheap and very clean. The owners are friendly and helpful; they seem to like us. They gave us drinks when we arrived and have told us about some places that we shouldn't miss. We plan to stay here in Ho Chi Minh City for a few days and visit temples in the city, then travel to the north.

pho

Reading Comprehension

Check Your Understanding

A Read the following sentences. Check (✔) true (*T*) or false (*F*). Then check the number of the post where you found the answer.

		T	F	①	②	③	④
1	In the past, Vietnam had an emperor.						
2	Many Hmong people speak English.						
3	This is Juliana's second trip to Vietnam.						
4	The market in Cholon has many kinds of vegetables.						
5	The town of Vung Tau is famous for its mountains.						

B Read the following sentences about Juliana's trip. Circle your answers. Then write the words or phrases from the reading that helped you find the answers.

1 She thinks the market in Cholon is really (great / expensive / noisy).

_____

2 She thinks the Hmong people are very (practical / modern / friendly).

_____

3 She likes hotels that are (expensive / traditional / simple).

_____

4 At the end of her trip, she says she wants to (go home and see her friends / visit more of Vietnam / learn to cook Vietnamese food).

_____

Critical Thinking

C Discuss the following questions with a partner.

1 How much money do you think Juliana and Tom spent on their trip? Why do you think so?

2 Do you blog about your travels? What other ways can you keep a record of your trips?

Vocabulary Comprehension

Odd Word Out

A Circle the word or phrase that does not belong in each group. The words in blue are from the passage.

1	accommodation	hotel	guesthouse	school
2	terrible	wonderful	fabulous	fantastic
3	tiring	relaxing	exhausting	demanding
4	similar	matching	unique	alike
5	possessions	belongings	plans	stuff
6	bored	interested	eager	fascinated
7	many kinds	range	alike	different
8	basic	advanced	easy	simple

B Complete the postcard using the words in blue from **A**.

Greetings from Madrid!
I can't believe I'm finally here. The trip from Seoul was long and
(1) _____, but I made it. My (2) _____ is
nice; I'm staying in a guesthouse in the center of Madrid. I got a
cheap and (3) _____ room—it only has a small bed
and shower! The weather here is (4) _____—it's
warm and sunny, with clear blue skies every day. It's great for
sightseeing, because there's a wide (5) _____ of
things to see and do. Tomorrow I'm taking a train south to An-
dalusia to visit the city of Granada. I'm really looking forward to
seeing the Alhambra Palace. I'm also really (6) _____
to try the food—especially gazpacho, a kind of cold soup which
I hear is (7) _____—very different from anything else
in Spain. I promise I'll bring you back a present. See you next month!

Love, Jamie

Plaza de Santa Ana 21

Madrid, Spain

26014

A Write the correct form of the adjectives in the box on the lines below.

> excite   interest   relax   confuse   please   embarrass   bore   worry

I feel . . . _excited_ _____

_____

because it's . . . _exciting_ _____

_____

B Change the verbs in the advertisement below into adjectives by using the correct endings.

EcoTours

Tired of going to the same **(1)** bor _____ places? **(2)** Interest
_____ in taking a vacation to an **(3)** excit _____ location?
Want a **(4)** relax _____ beach holiday, but also want to help save the
environment? If you answered "yes" to any of these questions, then you should book
your holiday with EcoTours! Not only will you experience the best vacation of your life,
but ten percent of the cost of your trip also goes to protecting the local environment.

Call us today to talk. Don't be **(5)** embarrass _____ to ask questions—
we want you to have the perfect vacation! If you are **(6)** worr_____
about the cost, don't be. Our prices are very reasonable. We know that you'll be
(7) pleas_____ with your EcoTours holiday, so give us a call at
(888) 555-3458, or visit us online to find out more at www.heinle-ecotours.org.

Vocabulary Skill
Adjective Endings -*ed* and -*ing*

> When we talk about how we feel, it's common to use adjectives that end in -*ed*. To describe something, or how we feel about it, use adjectives ending in -*ing*.

CHAPTER 2 Safe Travel

Before You Read
Preparing to Travel

A Think about answers to the following questions.

1 What are some risks or dangers of traveling abroad?

2 How can you prepare for a safe trip? What should you do during the trip?

B Discuss your answers with a partner.

Reading Skill
Predicting

> Before reading, think about what what you are going to read by looking at the title and any subheadings, and examining the images. While reading, you should also think about what comes next. This helps you understand a passage better.

A Look at the article on the next page. Read the title, the subheadings, and look at the pictures. Check (✔) advice you think the article will give. Discuss your answers with a partner.

1 ☐ learn basic phrases of the local language

2 ☐ go to local markets for cheap shopping

3 ☐ check the dates on your passport

4 ☐ keep your luggage close to you

5 ☐ walk instead of taking taxis to see more

6 ☐ book accommodation online for better prices

7 ☐ make sure you have the correct currency

B Skim the article to check your answers. Were your predictions correct?

C Now read the entire passage carefully. Then answer the questions on page 28.

> **Motivational Tip: Pause and think.** Before you answer the questions on page 28, pause and think. What was the most important information from this passage? How was it supported with examples? What do you now know that you didn't know before reading this passage? When we pause and think after we read, our comprehension will increase.

Safe Travel

Many travelers feel nervous about going to a new and unfamiliar place. If you plan your trip carefully and learn to take **precautions**, you can relax and enjoy yourself.

Check Your Paperwork[1]

5 While you prepare for your **departure,** make sure your paperwork is organized. You'll want to check the dates on your visas and passport. Having an important document **expire** before or during your trip is the last thing you want to happen. Be sure to get an international driver's license if you plan to drive while you are abroad. Also, do some research on the local currency. Some countries—
10 like Jamaica—use more than one currency. It's best to know how and when to use each.

Mind Your Health

If you need to take medication along, keep it in its original container. If you are carrying prescription[2] drugs, bring a letter from your doctor in case customs officials question you at your destination. Also, make sure that you travel with proper medical insurance so that if you are sick
15 or injured while traveling, you will be able to get treatment.

Pay Attention

As a tourist, you'll probably stand out on the street. Unlike local people, you'll carry guide books, refer to maps, take photos, and look up at buildings. Because of this, you may appear **vulnerable**.
20 Stay safe by keeping one eye on the amazing sights and the other on your personal items.

When you get into a taxi, make sure there is a meter[3] and that it is turned on. If there is no meter, agree on a price before starting out. Tour guides recommend protecting your luggage in busy transportation areas by always keeping it in front of you or
25 between your legs. Also, if you are going anywhere that requires **purchasing** tickets, be sure to buy them at an **authorized** location. Never purchase tickets on the street, as these are often overpriced, fake, or expired.

30 Learn About the Locals

It's always a good idea to buy a guide book and a map, and read about the local culture of the country you will be visiting. For example, it's important to know that in India you should use the right hand to eat, or to give and accept things. In Thailand, it's rude to point with your feet at someone or something. Also, try to learn a few basic words and phrases of the local language.
35 Don't **assume** that everyone will speak your language or that they will understand English.

If you have trouble communicating, look for students and young people who might speak a foreign language. And remember to smile. It's the friendliest and most **sincere** form of communication, and is understood everywhere in the world!

---

[1] Official documents like forms and reports are all **paperwork**.
[2] A **prescription** is a medicine that a doctor has told you to take.
[3] A **meter** is a machine that measures and records the amount of something.

Reading Comprehension
Check Your Understanding

A Read the following sentences. Check (✔) true (**T**) or false (**F**).

		T	F
1	It is important to be prepared, as well as careful, when you travel abroad.		
2	You usually can't use your country's money when you travel abroad.		
3	You should get insurance so that you can drive when you are overseas.		
4	You should bring a letter from your travel agent if you carry prescription drugs.		
5	It's rude to point at things with your feet in India.		

B Write advice given by the article for each situation.

1 You have a problem communicating in the local language.

_____

2 You get sick or have an accident.

_____

3 You want to take a taxi during your trip.

_____

4 You want to buy tickets to a theater show while on your trip.

_____

Critical Thinking

C Discuss the following questions with a partner.

1 Which tips from the article would you give to visitors to your country? Why?
2 Write two more safety tips for tourists who want to visit your country.

Vocabulary Comprehension
Words in Context

A Choose the best answer. The words in blue are from the passage.

1 What is something you can purchase?
  a a pair of shoes   **b** an idea

2 Which of the following will expire?
  a a visa   **b** luggage

3 Someone who is sincere is likely to tell _____.
  a lies   **b** the truth

4 Your flight's departure time is the time that your plane _____.
  a leaves the airport   **b** arrives at your destination

5 Which would need authorization?
  a applying for a passport   **b** eating at a restaurant

6 What is one precaution you can take against thieves?

    a Lock your doors.   **b** Call the police.

7 You see a woman holding a crying baby. What might you assume?

    a You talk to them.   **b** The woman is the child's mother.

8 Who is more vulnerable?

    a a baby   **b** an adult

B **Answer the following questions, then discuss your answers with a partner. The words in blue are from the passage.**

1 How can you tell when someone is being sincere?

2 How long before your departure time should you arrive at the airport?

3 What do you assume about people with a lot of money?

4 What are a few things that expire?

A Read the article below and (circle) all of the *pre-* words you find.

Travel Tips for San Francisco

1. Don't try to predict the weather. Bring a warm jacket and sweater so that you're prepared for changes in the temperature; even in the summer months of July and August, it gets cold.

2. Buy a prepaid phone card. Many of the phone booths at San Francisco airport and in the center of the city only accept prepaid calling cards.

3. Pre-arrange your hotel stay—especially in the summer months. Don't assume that it will be easy to find a room when you arrive. Hotels fill up quickly in San Francisco, particularly in the summer.

4. San Francisco is a great city for walking—but there are hills! Bring a comfortable pair of walking shoes if you're planning to go around on foot. Also, you can prevent stiff muscles by stretching, or avoiding the hills on the first day.

5. There are many wonderful cultural events happening in San Francisco all year round. Go online to get a preview of events happening at the time of your visit.

Vocabulary Skill
The Prefix *pre-*

In this chapter, you learned the noun *precaution*, a word made by combining the prefix *pre-*, meaning *done before* or *in advance*, with the noun *caution*, meaning *care*. *Pre-* can be combined with nouns, verbs, adjectives, and root words to form many words in English.

B **Write a *pre-* word from A for each definition below. Can you think of any other words that begin with *pre-*? Share your answers with a partner.**

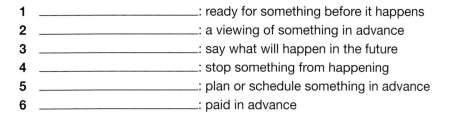

1 _____: ready for something before it happens

2 _____: a viewing of something in advance

3 _____: say what will happen in the future

4 _____: stop something from happening

5 _____: plan or schedule something in advance

6 _____: paid in advance

Real Life Skill

Reading and Understanding Immigration Forms

When you arrive in a foreign country, you must complete an immigration form to give to officials. These forms are for personal information, and they are often written in English.

A Read the immigration form below. Match the type of information with the question.

1 _____ given name
2 _____ gender
3 _____ marital status
4 _____ occupation
5 _____ citizenship
6 _____ permanent address
7 _____ date of birth
8 _____ surname

a Are you male or female?
b What's your job?
c What's your first name?
d What's your family name?
e Are you married?
f What's your nationality?
g When were you born?
h Where do you live?

Visitor Arrival Form

Surname: _____   Given name(s): _____

Passport Number: _____   Date of expiry: _____

Place of issue: _____

Permanent address: _____

_____

Date of birth: ____/____/____   Gender: M F Marital status: _____

Citizenship: _____

Occupation: _____

Purpose of stay: tourism _____ business _____ visit relatives _____ other _____

Length of stay: _____ days

Welcome to our country!

B Complete the form with information about yourself.

What do you think?

1 Do you read blogs written by other travelers before going on holiday? Did you find them useful?
2 Where have you traveled? Which place did you feel safest? Why?
3 What would you do if you were in trouble in a foreign country?

Getting Ready

Discuss the following questions with a partner.

1 What is the best movie you've seen in the last year? What did you like about it?
2 Have you ever wanted to work in the movies? Which jobs have you heard of?
3 Do you think making a movie is difficult? Why, or why not?

CHAPTER 1 Behind the Scenes

Before You Read
Making a Movie

A Think about answers to the following questions.

1 Why do you think it usually costs so much money to make a movie?
2 What kinds of jobs are needed to make a movie? Why are these jobs important?

B Discuss your answers with a partner.

Reading Skill
Using Headings to Understand Main Ideas

Looking at the title and the subheadings before you read can help you to understand what the main ideas of the reading will be.

A Look at the title and subheadings of the passage on the next page. Then (circle) the correct word or phrase in each of the main ideas below.

1 Makeup artists help the actors and actresses (sound great / look different).
2 The prop master gets (objects / money) needed for the movie.
3 The special effects coordinator creates things that (are / are not) real.
4 Foley artists work with the things you (hear / see) in a movie.

B Now read the entire passage to see if your answers in **A** were correct.

C Read the passage again carefully. Then answer the questions on page 34.

Motivational Tip: Sit in a different seat today. In most classrooms, students sit in the same seat near their friends. Today, I challenge you today to sit in a different seat, next to someone you don't know very well. In this class, when invited by your teacher, share what you are learning from today's chapter with your new partner.

Behind the Scenes

Who makes movies? Actors and **directors**, of course. But if you watch the **credits** at the end of a movie, you'll find hundreds of other names and jobs. Most of the **crucial** people in filmmaking aren't famous because they do their work behind the scenes[1]. Here are four important jobs. 5

Makeup artist: Making characters look believable

The makeup artist's work sounds simple, but there's more to it than making the lead actress look beautiful. If the hero gets a cut on his face, the makeup artist must create that cut and ensure it looks exactly the

10 same tomorrow and the day after. Some movies may require actors to look older or younger, or like a monster or a space alien. Putting on special makeup can sometimes take more time than the actor's scene! For example, Jim Carrey's makeup artist needed two and a half hours every day to **transform** him into his character for the movie, *The*

15 *Grinch*. The audience should notice the character, and not the makeup.

Property Master: Setting of scene

The property (or "prop") master is responsible for selecting parts of the set and costumes. This includes large items like furniture and vehicles, but also small items like tools and weapons. When you see a mother cooking breakfast for her kids, the prop master has chosen the stove, the frying pan, the plates, and almost everything else in the

20 **scene**. For a prop master, details are everything. In the 2011 movie *The Social Network*, the prop master had to find the exact model of computer that Facebook founder[2] Mark Zuckerberg used when he was studying at Harvard University back in 2004. Part of the job is also keeping track of every item purchased for the movie and making sure no item disappears during **production**.

Special effects coordinator: Making the impossible look real

After a movie, people often ask, "How did they do that?" In movies, 25 people can fly, dinosaurs roam through cities, and spaceships travel to other planets. These are all the work of the special effects coordinator. This person is responsible for creating fires and explosions, rainy days, or snowy nights. Most special effects nowadays are made with computers. A big movie like *Avatar* took 30 several years to make, and had many special effects companies working on different things. One company had about 120 people working **exclusively** on the look of the aliens on the planet Pandora.

Foley artist: Creating the sounds of the cinema

35 Think of your favorite scary movie and its sounds—footsteps, loud rain, and creaking doors. All of these are the work of the Foley artist. Many sounds can't be recorded during the filming of a movie, so Foley artists produce them in their **studios**. They create the punching and kicking sounds of a fight scene, and the wind, rain, and thunder in the background. They often have unexpected methods—for example, to make the sound of bones breaking, Foley artists have recorded the sound of celery sticks being snapped in half. In a Foley artist's studio, there might even be

40 special floors for recording different kinds of footsteps.

So next time you watch a film, be sure to look for these jobs in the credits. The movie wouldn't be the same without these hardworking people!

---

[1] People who work **behind the scenes** help to make a movie but do not appear in it.
[2] The **founder** of a company is the person who first started it.

Reading Comprehension

Check Your Understanding

A Read the following sentences. Check (✓) true (*T*) or false (*F*).

		T	F
1	The names of people who work behind the scenes are not in the movie credits.		
2	Movie makers want you to notice the great makeup when you watch a movie.		
3	A prop master decides which objects actors use in a movie.		
4	Special effects coordinators usually need computers for their job.		
5	Most of the sounds you hear in a movie are recorded during filming.		

B Who did it? Write the correct job for each movie scene.

1 _____ We hear a car accident outside the window.
2 _____ In a scene, a man sits in a car from the 1990s and uses a cell phone.
3 _____ The restaurant looks exactly the same in the next scene.
4 _____ The hero's skin looks green after he returns from his space flight.
5 _____ A fire starts in the family's kitchen.

Critical Thinking

C Discuss the following questions with a partner.

1 Which of these four jobs do you think is the most important in making a good movie? Why?
2 How do you think these people start out in their jobs? What kind of training would they need to have?

Vocabulary Comprehension

Definitions

A Match each word with its definition. The words in blue are from the passage.

1	____ director	a	very important
2	____ credits	b	one part of a movie
3	____ scene	c	a place where movies are made
4	____ crucial	d	a list of all the people who worked on a movie
5	____ production	e	the making of a movie
6	____ transform	f	to change completely
7	____ exclusive	g	involving only one specific thing
8	____ studio	h	the person who gives instructions to make a movie

B Answer the following questions, then discuss your answers with a partner. The words in blue are from the passage.

1 What is the scariest scene of any movie you've seen?
2 Do you think a good story is crucial to the success of a movie?
3 Which names are usually listed first in the credits of a movie?
4 Have you ever been to an exclusive event? What was it like?

A Use the prefix *dis-* and one of the words from the box to complete the definitions.

Vocabulary Skill
The Prefix *dis-*

In the passage *Behind the Scenes*, you saw the word *disappear*, a word made by combining the prefix *dis-*, meaning *not*, with the verb *appear*. The prefix *dis-* is placed at the beginning of a noun, verb, or adjective to make the word negative.

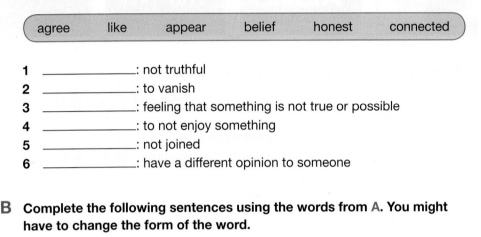

| agree | like | appear | belief | honest | connected |

1 _____: not truthful
2 _____: to vanish
3 _____: feeling that something is not true or possible
4 _____: to not enjoy something
5 _____: not joined
6 _____: have a different opinion to someone

B Complete the following sentences using the words from A. You might have to change the form of the word.

1 Many people _____ spicy food.
2 Now I know why the printer isn't working; it's _____!
3 Paul could only look at his girlfriend in _____ when she said she wanted to break up with him.
4 When the sun came out, the fog _____.
5 I don't trust that salesman. He looks really _____.
6 Jean and her husband fight a lot because they _____ on everything.

C Complete the following questions using the words from A. Take turns asking and answering the questions with a partner.

1 Which foods do you _____?
2 Have you ever met a _____ person?
3 Do you agree or _____ that it is possible to predict the future?
4 Can you make a coin _____?

CHAPTER 2 The Rise of J. J. Abrams

Before You Read
Who is J. J. Abrams?

A **Think about answers to the following questions.**

1 Have you seen any of these movies and television shows? Did you like them?

2 What do these movies and television shows have in common?

3 Do you know who J. J. Abrams is? Can you guess what he is famous for?

B **Discuss your answers with a partner.**

Reading Skill
Recognizing Sequence of Events

A **Read the following sentences about J. J. Abrams' life and career. Without reading the passage, put the events in order from 1–7. Compare your ideas with a partner.**

> Dates and times in a passage are often introduced with words like *first, then, next, when, in, today*, and *finally* to indicate the sequence of events. Recognizing the sequence, or order, of events can help you to understand the reading better.

1	When he was 11 or 12, Abrams' grandfather gave him a movie camera called a Super 8.
	His movie success caught the attention of top filmmaker Steven Spielberg.
	Abrams made his movie directing debut almost a decade later in 2006, with *Mission: Impossible III*.
	Not long after the camera, Abrams' grandfather gave him a box of magic tricks.
	His next move was into television in 1998, when he helped create the popular TV series *Felicity*.
	Today, the couple and their three children live near Los Angeles, California, where Abrams has his own production company called Bad Robot.
	He soon got his first opportunity at 16 years old, when he wrote music for a movie called *Nightbeast*.

B (Circle) **the words or numbers in the sentences that helped you choose the order. Then skim the entire passage to see if your answers in A were correct.**

C **Read the entire passage carefully. Then answer the questions on page 38.**

THE RISE OF J. J. ABRAMS

J. J. Abrams was born in New York City in 1966. Growing up, Abrams loved mysteries and magic tricks—anything that was unexpected. His favorite movies and television programs were science fiction ones like *The Twilight Zone*.

5   When he was 11 or 12, Abrams' grandfather gave him a movie camera called a Super 8. He used the camera to make short movies with his sister and their friends. From then on, Abrams' **ambition** was to work in Hollywood and make movies and TV shows. He soon got his
10 first opportunity at 16 years old, when he wrote music for a movie called *Nightbeast*.

In college, Abrams co-wrote and sold a screenplay to a Hollywood production company. He started gaining popularity for his work, and his next two dramas—*Regarding Henry* and *Forever*
15 *Young*—were hit movies. Abrams continued to write and produce screenplays throughout his 20s, the biggest being *Armageddon*.

But Abrams never lost his **passion** for the mysterious and wanted to create shows like the ones he enjoyed as a child. His next move was into television in 1998, when he helped create the popular TV series *Felicity*. Some of his shows became huge hits,
20 like the spy drama *Alias* and the Emmy-winning mystery thriller *Lost*. Abrams made his movie directing **debut** almost a decade later in 2006, with *Mission: Impossible III*. He then went on to direct the science fiction movie *Star Trek* in 2009. His movie success caught the attention of top filmmaker Steven Spielberg. Together, they created the monster movie *Super 8*, named for the camera both men experimented with when
25 they were young.

The Super 8 camera has proved to be very **influential** in Abrams' life, but there is another special gift that has helped Abrams become who he is today. Not long after the camera, Abrams' grandfather gave him a box of magic tricks. Abrams calls it a "mystery box," because he never opened it. He says he wants to **preserve** the mystery, and remind
30 himself to create unexpected stories. To him, the box "**represents** infinite[1] possibility. It represents hope. It represents potential."

Abrams has even used the box **metaphor** to describe movie theaters. "What's a bigger mystery box than a movie theater? You go to the theater, you're just so excited to see anything…mystery boxes are everywhere in what I do." The box remains a source of
35 **inspiration** for Abrams, and he keeps it on a shelf in his office.

At a dinner party in 1994, Abrams met a woman named Katie McGrath and they got married soon after. Today, the couple and their three children live near Los Angeles, California, where Abrams runs his own production company called Bad Robot. He keeps busy, usually working on many projects at once, and is always looking to create
40 more and more mystery boxes.

---

[1] Something that is infinite has no limits or boundaries in time, space, size, etc.

Reading Comprehension
Check Your Understanding

A Choose the correct answers for the following questions.

1 What kind of passage is this?
   a a biography   b a newspaper article   c a critical review

2 What can be understood from the passage?
   a J.J. Abrams is no longer making movies.
   b J.J. Abrams has opened the magic box.
   c J.J. Abrams still enjoys making entertainment.

3 Abrams compares _____ to his box of magic tricks.
   a the love of a boy and his grandfather
   b the mystery of going to a movie theater
   c watching mystery television shows

B Read the following sentences. Check (✓) true (*T*) or false (*F*).

		T	F
1	Abrams mostly wrote screenplays in his 20s.		
2	Abrams compares the movie theater to his Super 8 camera.		
3	Steven Spielberg has worked with Abrams since Abrams' television days.		
4	Abrams works for his wife's production company, Bad Robot.		
5	Abrams likes to work on more than one project at a time.		

Critical Thinking

C Discuss the following questions with a partner.

1 What else could you compare a movie theater to? Why?
2 Would you open the mystery box if you were Abrams? Why, or why not?

Vocabulary Comprehension
Words in Context

A Choose the best answer. The words in blue are from the passage.

1 The color red usually represents _____.
   a danger   b something easily noticed

2 The main ambition of many professional athletes is to _____.
   a win competitions   b stay healthy

3 Someone who has passion for something usually spends _____ time doing it.
   a very little   b a lot of

4 An influential person would most likely be _____ by other people.
   a ignored   b listened to

5 People usually want to preserve _____ things.
   a good   b bad

6 You usually get inspiration from people you _____.
   a admire   b dislike

7 Which is a metaphor?

    a Life is a journey.   **b** My mother likes flowers.

8 An actor's debut is the _____ of his or her career.

    a start   **b** end

B **Complete the following sentences with the words in blue from A. You might have to change the form of the words.**

1 I spent a lot of money on my bike because I'm _____ about cycling. My _____ is to become a professional cyclist one day.

2 The band's new song is pretty good, but I still prefer music from their _____ album.

3 My mother thinks my new friend is a bad _____ on me.

4 I hope developers will _____ some of the old buildings in the area, instead of knocking them all down.

A **One way to organize words is to categorize them by part of speech. Write _N_ (nouns), _V_ (verbs), or _A_ (adjectives) next to the following words. Then review their meanings with a partner.**

____ director	____ create	____ scene	____ scary	____ script
____ studio	____ credits	____ avoid	____ disappear	____ Hollywood
____ produce	____ hero	____ important	____ lead	____ actress
____ impossible	____ prepare	____ supervisor	____ famous	____ monster

B **You can also organize words by meaning, for example, nouns for people, places, and things. Organize the nouns from A into one of these categories.**

People	Places	Things

Vocabulary Skill
Organizing Vocabulary

One helpful way to remember new words is to group them into meaningful categories, for example, by part of speech or by topic. Organizing your vocabulary can also help you to relate new vocabulary to other words you know.

Motivational Tip: Reading for pleasure. As a class, discuss what you are reading for pleasure—not because you are assigned to read it but because you want to. When you choose to make reading a regular part of your life, you will find greater levels of satisfaction.

Real Life Skill

Understanding the Use of Italics

Italics are used to distinguish certain words in a text from the others. We commonly use italics to emphasize or stress a word or phrase (I am *not* going), to set apart a word from others (What does *station* mean?), and to identify titles of books, newspapers, magazines, and movies.

A Why are italics used in each example below? Write *a*, *b*, or *c*.

> **a** to set apart a word from others
> **b** to emphasize or stress a word
> **c** to identify a title

1 _____ J. J. Abrams has been nominated many times for an Emmy Award, but he has only *won* once.

2 _____ *The Twilight Zone* was a very popular science fiction television show.

3 _____ Words like *first*, *second*, *then, next, later,* and *finally* indicate a sequence of events.

B Why are italics used in the movie review below? Explain your answers to a partner.

> ### New Movie *The Spirits* Opens to Glowing Reviews
>
> *Scary* and *exciting* are words that *Big Screen* magazine and viewers around the country are using to describe the movie *The Spirits*, which opened today in theaters everywhere. Set in a village outside London at the end of World War II, the movie tells the story of a woman living in a house visited by ghosts from the war. The movie is based on the book *The Haunting of Powell Manor* by Robert Johnston.
>
> "I was really impressed," said moviegoer Diana Owens of Los Angeles. "It's a ghost story that will keep you guessing and jumping. At one point, a scene in the movie was so scary that *everyone* in the theater screamed." There's also a surprise ending to the story. "I won't tell you what it is," said Owens, "but pay attention to the word *invitation* in the movie."

C Write sentences of your own to show the three different uses of italics. (Circle) the words that should be in italics.

1 _____

2 _____

3 _____

What do you think?

1 If you could work in the movie industry, what job would you want to do? Why?

2 J. J. Abrams was inspired by a Super 8 camera. Do you have anything that inspires you?

3 What makes a movie timeless? Which movies will people still enjoy 20 years from now? Why do you think so?

Fluency Strategy: PRO

PRO stands for **P**review, **R**ead, **O**rganize. This reading strategy will help you build your reading fluency by helping you to organize and understand what you read.

Preview

The first stage of PRO is to **preview** the reading material by looking for features of the text that can help you. Read the title of the passage and any other **headings**. If any words in the passage are written in *italics*, read them. Read the **first paragraph**, the **first sentences in the middle paragraphs**, and the **final paragraph**. After doing this, stop for a minute and think about what the reading is about. Think about what you already know about the topic, and any questions you have that you hope the passage can answer.

Preview the reading passage on the next page, *Are Human Beings Getting Smarter*? What do you think the answer to the title question will be? Then skim the rest of the passage and write a list of questions you hope to answer as you read the passage in detail.

Read

Now, **read** *Are Human Beings Getting Smarter*? When you read, think about the questions you listed in the Preview stage. Look for answers to your questions.

Organize

The final stage of PRO is to **organize** the information in some way that will help you remember what you have read. One way is by creating a word web. The word web can help you easily see how the information in the passage is organized.

A **Here is an incomplete word web based on *Are Human Beings Getting Smarter*? Complete the rest of the word web using the information in the passage.**

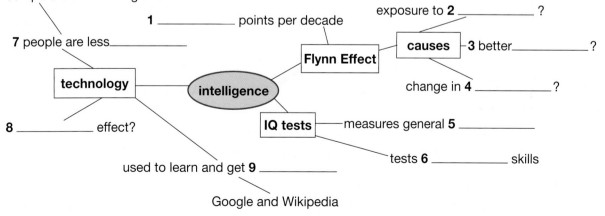

computers and video games

7 people are less_____

1 _____ points per decade

exposure to **2** _____ ?

causes —**3** better_____?

Flynn Effect

change in **4** _____?

technology

intelligence

8 _____ effect?

IQ tests — measures general **5** _____

tests **6** _____ skills

used to learn and get **9** _____

Google and Wikipedia

Are Human Beings Getting Smarter?

Do you think you're smarter than your parents and grandparents? According to James Flynn, a professor at a New Zealand university, you might be. Over the course of the last century, IQ test scores of people in some countries have gotten increasingly better—on average, three points better for every decade that has passed. This trend of improving
5   scores is known as "the Flynn effect," and scientists want to know what is behind it.

IQ tests and other similar tests are designed to measure general intelligence rather than knowledge. Flynn knew that intelligence is partly inherited from our parents and partly the result of our environment and experiences, but the improvement in test scores was happening too quickly to be explained by heredity.[1] So what happened in
10 the 20th century that led to higher test scores?

Scientists have proposed several explanations for the Flynn effect. Some suggest that the improved test scores simply reflect an increased exposure to tests in general. Because we take so many tests, we learn test-taking techniques that help us perform better. Others have pointed to better nutrition, which results in babies being born
15 larger, healthier, and with more brain development than in the past. Another possible explanation is a change in educational styles—children are encouraged to discover things for themselves rather than just memorizing information. This could prepare people to do the kind of problem-solving that intelligence tests require.

Flynn himself suggested that learning new technologies may have improved people's
20 problem-solving skills. This may be true for the first decade of his tests, when IQ scores in many countries increased. However, in recent years, IQ test scores in some countries have begun to decline. Data from Norway, the Netherlands, Australia, and Great Britain have shown that as these countries become more and more modern, IQ scores have begun to drop.

25 While scientists aren't sure what's causing this decline, they think technology is dramatically changing the way that we learn and get information. For example, people are now able to access all kinds of information very easily using online resources like Google or Wikipedia. The danger is when they start to rely too much on these sources of information, and not do any thinking for themselves. Lifestyle changes that come with modern
30 technology may also have a negative effect on intelligence, such as video games and television making people less social. So while the world may have gotten smarter over the 20th century, improving technology and changing lifestyles may soon reverse that trend.

---

[1] **Heredity** is the process by which features and characteristics are passed on to you from your parents through your genes.

B **Choose the best answer for the following questions. Use the word web from A to help you.**

1 What best describes the Flynn effect?
   a a way to measure intelligence
   b an increase in IQ test scores
   c a way of teaching university students
   d an explanation for why people are less smart

2 The Flynn effect is probably the result of _____ .
   a heredity
   b our environment and experiences
   c taking fewer tests
   d memorizing information

3 IQ tests evaluate our _____ .
   a knowledge
   b environment
   c intelligence
   d memories

4 Who does *others* in line 14 refer to?
   a babies
   b scientists
   c people in general
   d people who take tests

5 Which sentence gives the main idea of the passage?
   a This trend of improving scores is known as "the Flynn effect," and scientists want to know what is behind it.
   b Because we take so many tests, we learn test-taking techniques that help us perform better.
   c However, in recent years, IQ test scores in some countries have begun to decline.
   d Lifestyle changes that come with modern technology may also have a negative effect on intelligence.

6 The writer uses video games as an example of how _____ .
   a we are becoming less social
   b technology increases problem-solving skills
   c people don't think for themselves
   d countries are becoming more technologically advanced

7 Which statement would the writer probably agree with?
   a People today are more intelligent in every way.
   b People today have fewer problems to solve.
   c People today don't take enough tests.
   d People today use computers too much.

SELF CHECK

Answer the following questions.

1 Have you ever used the PRO method before?

☐ Yes ☐ No ☐ I'm not sure.

2 Will you practice PRO in your reading outside of English class?

☐ Yes ☐ No ☐ I'm not sure.

3 Do you think PRO is helpful? Why, or why not?

_____

_____

4 Which of the six reading passages in units 1–3 did you enjoy most? Why?

_____

_____

5 Which of the six reading passages in units 1–3 was easiest? Which was most difficult? Why?

_____

_____

6 What have you read in English outside of class recently?

_____

_____

7 What distractions do you face when you read? What can you do to minimize those distractions?

_____

_____

8 How will you try to improve your reading fluency from now on?

_____

_____

Reading Review 1: The Film and the Novel: *Twilight*

Fluency Practice

Time yourself as you read through the passage. Try to read as fluently as you can. Record your time in the Reading Rate Chart on page 176. Then answer the questions on page 46.

The Film and the Novel: *Twilight*

1 When a popular book gets made into a movie, there will always be a debate about whether the novel or film is better. The filmmakers always have to consider certain things: do they want to follow the book closely to please dedicated readers, or do they want to change
5 parts of the book if they don't translate well on-screen? No matter what they do, there will always be people who feel the movie will never be as good as the book, people who will love the movie without ever reading the book, and people who enjoy both.

2 The vampire series *Twilight*, by Stephenie Meyer, became so popular
10 that movie companies wanted to produce it for the big screen. Most *Twilight* fans were excited about seeing characters such as Edward and Bella "come to life," but there were other fans who did not trust the movie script. They assumed the scriptwriters would change parts of the story to make it seem more interesting as a movie.

3 15 By the time the first *Twilight* movie was released, millions of people had read the series. Many of these people went on to watch the film, which made $35.7 million just on its opening day. While many fans and critics liked it and said the movie more or less followed the book's storyline, some fans were not impressed. One change that angered
20 them was that certain sound effects were added to the movie, such as a "whooshing" sound when the vampires jumped. This was not mentioned in the book, and many fans felt that it was too distracting.

4 Those who liked the movie said they enjoyed the light mood and excitement. This was very different from the book. The writing in
25 *Twilight* is dark and gloomy, like many vampire novels. The movie, however, added more energy to the story and more personality to the characters. For example, many characters in the book are portrayed as being quiet, and they spend most of their time at school. But in the movie, the characters are cooler and funnier—one scene even shows
30 them going surfing together. The director of the first movie, Catherine Hardwicke, thought it was important for the characters to be believable. She wanted **them** to have a wide variety of emotions, since the series is for, and about, teenagers.

5 In the end, the films were considered a success, even if there were both happy and unhappy fans. It's a great accomplishment to make films that are watched by millions of people, and you can't
35 expect to be able to please everyone all of the time.

431 words   **Time taken** _____

Reading Comprehension

1 What is the main idea of the first paragraph?
   a It takes a long time to make books into movies.
   b Filmmakers prefer to make movies out of popular books.
   c People will always compare movies to the books.
   d Many people will see a movie without reading the book.

2 Why does the passage say fans were excited to see the movie?
   a to see how the story would change
   b to see which actors would play their favorite characters
   c to see real people acting out the story
   d to see if the movie would be better than the book

3 The passage discusses vampires jumping _____ .
   a as an example of a sound effect
   b as an example of a change that displeased fans
   c because it was a special effect and not real
   d to say how scary the movie was

4 The book *Twilight* is described as very _____ .
   a exciting
   b serious
   c fun
   d funny

5 According to the passage, what was NOT changed for the movie?
   a storyline
   b mood
   c characters
   d sound effects

6 In line 31, *them* refers to the _____ .
   a directors
   b actors
   c characters
   d fans

7 What best describes this passage?
   a a comparison of a book and a movie
   b a review of a movie
   c an introduction to a book
   d a discussion of how books are made into movies

Reading Review 2: Organic Farming: The New Vacation

Organic Farming: The New Vacation

1   In 1971, Sue Coppard worked as a secretary in London. While she enjoyed city life, Sue also missed the countryside where she spent most of her time as a child. So
5   she offered to help out on a farm, or more specifically, an organic farming program organized by a nearby college. She got a few people to volunteer as well, and they spent the weekend doing "housework,"
10 which involved clearing bushes and cleaning drains. Afterwards, the farm managers said they could come back anytime to help out.

2   Sue put a small ad in a magazine, offering people the chance to volunteer at the organic farm. The volunteer program grew quickly, and soon other organic farmers joined in, asking for people to help out. With so many people and farms involved, someone needed to **organize** the different groups. A few of
15 the original volunteers started WWOOF (World Wide Opportunities on Organic Farms) to help volunteers and farmers find one another. Today, at least 50 different countries have WWOOF organizations, and many other countries have individual farms that participate in the movement.

3   While WWOOF is still a weekend activity for some, it now welcomes travelers and people who wish to live and work on farms for longer periods of time. WWOOF volunteers can stay on a farm for weeks or
20 even months at a time in exchange for hands-on farming and gardening experience. The work can be exhausting, but volunteers think it's worth it. By working on farms, the volunteers interact with farmers and develop a love for the outdoors and organic farming. Many travelers now use WWOOFing as a way to visit new countries and experience new cultures.

4   As travelers will discover, every WWOOF opportunity is a bit different. In Serbia, you can find Misa and
25 Olja, a couple whose farm is known for its hard cheeses and for its bread made from homegrown grains. Finca Amiruca, a farm in Ecuador, teaches volunteers how to grow peanuts, plantains, and yucca. When volunteering in Japan, you may get to learn about growing rice.

5   WWOOF is only one of the many unique volunteer opportunities available. Volunteering is something that anyone can do, and a wide variety of organizations accept or even welcome volunteers. So the next time
30 you get the itch to be active on the weekend or on vacation, why not look for a good cause to spend your energy on?

400 words   Time taken _____

Reading Comprehension

1 Why did Sue first work on a farm?
    a She was a student at the university.
    b She needed money.
    c She missed the countryside.
    d She did not enjoy her job.

2 More people joined the program when Sue _____ .
    a put an advertisement in a magazine
    b hung posters at a school
    c asked friends and neighbors to come
    d offered to pay people to work

3 In line 14, the word *organize* means _____ .
    a pay
    b arrange
    c cancel
    d work

4 When living on a WWOOF farm, volunteers _____ .
    a must pay the farm's owner
    b can stay for a long or short time
    c are given a special bedroom
    d sleep outdoors

5 Which is NOT a change that WWOOF has undergone since it first started?
    a It has spread to many different countries.
    b It has many more people volunteering for it.
    c It allows people to stay for longer periods of time.
    d It is less tiring than it used to be.

6 What is special about the farm in Serbia?
    a It is the only farm in the country where rice is grown.
    b Peanuts, plantains, and yucca are grown on the farm.
    c It is an animal farm, with lots of pigs and cattle.
    d The people at the farm make cheese and bread.

7 What is the purpose of the last paragraph?
    a to introduce a new volunteer organization
    b to explain why working on a farm is good
    c to give one more detail about WWOOF
    d to encourage readers to volunteer

Young Athletes

Getting Ready

Discuss the following questions with a partner.

1 Can you name the sports above? Write their names in the boxes. What other sports do you know?
2 Which athletes do you think are the best in their sport?
3 Do you know of any young athletes? How old were they when they first started?

Before You Read
Setting Records

A Read the following about a day in the life of a college football player.

6 AM:	Wake up and get ready for the day. I have a banana and a slice of toast with peanut butter to give me energy for my morning exercise.
7 AM:	A run around the lake, followed by lifting weights at the gym. Every athlete knows that being fit is one of the keys to being a good player.
8 AM:	Breakfast – I'm so hungry! This is an athlete's most important meal of the day, so we make sure to have a big one. I usually have five eggs with spinach and tomatoes, and a big cup of coffee.
9 AM:	Classes start.
12 noon:	Lunch with friends.
1 PM:	More classes, followed by private tuition. We sometimes miss classes because we travel across the country for games, so we have tutors to help us catch up on our studies.
4 PM:	Football training starts. We do our warm-ups, then move on to exercises and practice games. The National Championships are coming up, so we train extra hard.
7:30 PM:	Dinner with the team. It's all football talk!
9 PM:	Back to our dorms, where I work on my class paper and watch TV.
11 PM:	Bed time. I try to get seven hours of sleep every night, which isn't difficult because I'm so tired by the end of the day!

B Discuss the following questions with a partner.

1 How are athletes' lives different from a normal student's? Would you want to be a young athlete?
2 When should an athlete start playing a sport if he or she wants to be famous? Does it matter?

Reading Skill
Previewing

Previewing involves skills like skimming, scanning, and predicting in preparation for reading a new passage. Ask yourself questions like: *What is this about? What kind of text is this? What do I already know about it?*

A Take one minute to preview the reading passage. Think about the title and the picture, scan the passage for interesting information, and skim the first and last paragraph.

B Now discuss the following questions with a partner.

1 What do you think the passage is about?
2 What do you already know about this subject?
3 What is interesting or special about Laura Dekker?

C Read the entire passage carefully. Then answer the questions on page 52.

Laura Dekker: Record-Setter!

All athletes **aspire** to be the best in their sport, and young athletes are no different. More young athletes now aim to win
5 competitions, set records, or perform amazing **feats**. And some, like Dutch sailor Laura Dekker, achieve that **goal**.

As a child, Laura Dekker loved
10 the sea. She was born on a boat in New Zealand, and has hardly stepped off one since. Laura first sailed by herself at age six, displaying a **talent** for understanding her boat and the confidence to control it. At 13 years old, Laura felt ready for the biggest challenge of all: she wanted to set the **record** for the youngest person ever to sail around the world alone.

Before she could do that, she had to face many challenges. While her parents were
15 confident that she could do it, the Dutch government tried to stop her, arguing that she was too young to risk her life. Many people also felt that she should be focusing on her studies. After a long battle, she finally got permission. She had to go for classes to learn how to care for herself while alone at sea, and had to use a bigger boat than she was used to. To avoid falling behind in her studies, she had to sign up with a special
20 distance-learning school and promise to do her homework at sea.

Finally, at the age of 15, Laura was ready. On January 20, 2011, she set out from the island of St. Maarten in the Caribbean on her 38-foot (11.5-meter) sailboat, *Guppy*. Her trip lasted 500 days in total, partly because she had to stop at different ports to study and check her boat. During this time, she visited **exotic** islands like the Galápagos, Bora Bora, and Vanuatu,
25 and also found time to go surfing, scuba diving, and cliff diving. She even discovered a new hobby: playing the flute! Laura was alone for most of her journey, but she kept a blog that was read by many people around the world.

Laura returned to St. Maarten at the age of 16 years and 123 days, and was greeted by her family, friends, and many fans. She had become the youngest sailor to circle the globe alone.
30 However, Guinness World Records and the World Sailing Speed Record Council did not **verify** her claim, saying they no longer recognize records for youngest sailors because it could encourage other young people to do dangerous things. Despite this, Laura felt a sense of **achievement**. She said that spending so much time alone on her trip helped her to focus on the important things in her life. "I became good friends with my boat," Laura said.
35 "I learned a lot about myself."

CHAPTER 2 The Unbeatable Yani Tseng

Before You Read
Sports Personalities

Venus and Serena
Williams, tennis players

Usain Bolt, sprinter

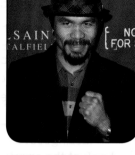

Manny Pacquaio,
boxer

A Think about answers to the following questions.

1 Do you recognize the athletes above? What do you know about them?
2 Who is your favorite athlete? Do you like that person because of their sports ability or because of their personality?
3 Do you think having an interesting personality helps an athlete? Why?

B Discuss your answers with a partner.

Reading Skill
Predicting

> When we know the topic of a passage, we can use it to predict the kind of words or information we might read. Using this skill can help us to understand what we will read about.

A Look at the title and picture in the passage on the next page. The passage is about a female athlete who became very successful at a young age. Check (✓) what you think the passage will mention.

☐ physical strength
☐ the right body type
☐ the right personality
☐ a supportive family

☐ good luck
☐ good coaches and training
☐ hard work
☐ lots of money

B Now skim the passage to see if your answers in **A** were correct.

C Read the entire passage carefully. Then answer the questions on page 56.

The Unbeatable Yani Tseng

Yani Tseng is one of the brightest stars of the golfing world, not to mention a superstar in Taiwan, where she grew up. By the age of 22, she had achieved things most golfers can only dream of. She had been named LPGA Player of the Year
5 twice, and was the youngest **professional** golfer—male or female—to win five major **tournaments.**

Yani started playing golf when she was very young, thanks to her **enthusiastic** parents who are both golfers. Her father gave her a set of golf clubs when she was only five years old. At 13 years
10 old, she told him she wanted to take up golf as an occupation. Just one year later, Yani won the Callaway Junior World Golf Championships and went on to become the top **amateur** player in Taiwan. She finally started playing in professional tournaments when she was 18 years old, and then her career really took off.

15 Brittany Lang, who came second to Yani at the Women's British Open in 2011, calls her "unbelievable." She says Yani is "so mentally strong and she's so **aggressive** and confident. She's just got it all. It's pretty cool to watch."

But Yani was not always so confident, especially off the golf course. When she first left her home to start playing in international tournaments, she didn't speak English very well. She struggled to
20 communicate with other golfers and had to use an interpreter[1] for interviews. Because she was shy about her English, Yani had a reputation[2] as a very quiet person. Yani's **coach**, Gary Gilchrist, says that studying English has helped Yani change this. "She worked so hard to improve her English," said Gilchrist. "Now her confidence is a 9 on a scale of 10."

Today, Yani is well known for her big smile and **sense of humor**. She loves to chat and joke
25 with reporters, fans, and other golfers. Once, before a tournament near her home in Florida, Yani invited a number of golfers and golf reporters to her place for a dinner party. Halfway through the party, she decided to dress up as Harry Potter, and even gave a speech wearing her black coat and round spectacles.

As a teenager, Yani looked up to adult golfers like Annika Sorenstam and saw them as her **role**
30 **models.** Today, she herself hopes to inspire young girls to take up golf, the same way Sorenstam influenced a whole generation of women golfers. Yani is also an inspiration to people trying to pick up English. Her advice to English learners: "Keep talking. I'm not afraid to be talking to other people, no matter what I say. I'm learning from the way [I talk] to you, and the vocabulary, I use it for the next time [I talk]."

[1] An **interpreter** is someone who translates from one language to another.
[2] Your **reputation** is the opinion people have of you.

Reading Comprehension
Check Your Understanding

A Choose the correct answers for the following questions.

1 Which event happened first?
  a Yani began playing golf.
  b Yani moved to the United States.
  c Yani turned 13.

2 How did Yani change after learning English?
  a She became more confident.
  b She began studying other languages.
  c She became more interested in golf.

3 Which is NOT mentioned as helping Yani speak better English?
  a She talks to people in English.
  b She learns vocabulary and tries to use it.
  c She takes lessons with her interpreter.

B Read the following sentences. Check (✓) true (T) or false (F).

		T	F
1	Yani won major tournaments before she turned professional.		
2	Yani's parents supported her interest in playing golf.		
3	Brittany Lang beat Yani in the Women's British Open.		
4	Yani asked people to dress up as Harry Potter for her party.		
5	Annika Sorenstam says Yani is one of her role models.		

Critical Thinking

C Discuss the following questions with a partner.

1 Do you think athletes make good role models? Why, or why not?

2 Do you think athletes should always be serious during competitions? Why, or why not?

Vocabulary Comprehension
Words in Context

A Choose the best answer. The words in blue are from the passage.

1 _____ athletes play their sport for money.
  a Amateur   **b** Professional

2 Athletes _____ during a tournament.
  a relax   **b** compete *competition*

3 The coach of a sports team usually has _____ experience than the players.
  a more   **b** less

4 Jenny is known for her sense of humor. She _____ a lot.
  a argues   **b** laughs

5 A person who is enthusiastic to start a project is _____ by the work.
  a bored   **b** excited

6 People generally _____ talking to an aggressive person.

    a like   **b** don't like

7 A role model is someone you _____.

    a respect   **b** fear

B Complete the following paragraph with the words in blue from **A**. You might have to change the form of the word.

Young player leads his team to 4–3 victory

16-year-old Paulo Dias led the Metro City Rangers to victory last night in the final game of the National Soccer **(1)** _____ when he scored a goal in the last minute. The team's **(2)** _____, Ray Palmer, said, "We're very happy with Paulo. He's young but has great talent. He's very soft-spoken in person, but can be **(3)** _____ on the pitch and isn't afraid to challenge bigger players." Dias is **(4)** _____ about his future in football and says that one day he'd like to play on a **(5)** _____ team like his **(6)** _____, Lionel Messi. "Next year, I'll be even better and stronger!" Dias promised.

A Use the suffix *-ous* to change the nouns in the chart to adjectives. Use your dictionary to help you with spelling.

Noun	Adjective	Noun	Adjective
humor		courage	
danger		nerve	
fame		adventure	

Vocabulary Skill

Adjectives with the Suffix *-ous*

> One way of forming adjectives in English is to combine *-ous* with a noun. The suffix *-ous* means *to have* or *to be full of*.

B Complete the following questions using one of the adjectives from **A**. Some may have more than one answer. Then discuss the questions with a partner.

1 Do you consider yourself a(n) _____ person? Why?

2 Have you ever met a(n) _____ person?

3 What's the most _____ thing you have ever done?

4 Have you ever been in a(n) _____ situation? What happened?

5 Can you make people laugh? Do you know any _____ stories or jokes?

> **Motivational Tip: Why is this reading skill important?** You will practice this reading skill in this chapter, but where can you also use this skill? When you realize that a reading skill can be applied beyond the text, your reading will improve.

CHAPTER 1 You Are Amazing: You Are Human!

Before You Read
Do You Know Your Body?

A Read the following sentences and check (✔) true (*T*) or false (*F*).

		T	F
1	Your ability to hear is reduced if you eat too much.		
2	Men have a better sense of smell than women.		
3	You are taller in the morning than you are at night.		
4	Nails and hair continue to grow after we die.		
5	Your brain is more active during the day than at night.		
6	Humans are the only animals that cry when upset		

B Discuss your answers with a partner. Then check your answers at the bottom of page 61.

Reading Skill
Identifying Main Ideas within Paragraphs

> Every paragraph has a main idea, or topic, which gives us the most important information in that paragraph. The main idea is often mentioned in the beginning or concluding sentence of the paragraph.

A Skim the first paragraph on the next page. (Circle) the sentence that describes the main idea. Discuss your answer with a partner.

  a Many facts about your body are surprising.
  b Your body is mostly made of water.

B Skim the rest of the paragraphs. (Circle) the main idea for each paragraph.

Paragraph 2
  a Your body is very complicated, like a machine.
  b Your body can develop many different problems.

Paragraph 3
  a Stress can cause many health problems.
  b We do many things that can damage our bodies.

Paragraph 4
  a Doctors can treat many health problems that come with old age.
  b Modern medicine helps people live much longer than in the past.

Paragraph 5
  a The most important habit for good health is regular exercise.
  b We can do many things to take care of our bodies.

C Now read the entire passage carefully. Then answer the questions on page 62.

You Are Amazing: You Are Human!

1 Did you know that your small intestine is nearly six meters long? Or that there are about 60 muscles in your face, and you use 40 of them to frown[1] but only 20 to smile? How about the fact that our bodies **consist of** 73 percent water, and that our hearts beat over 100,000 times each day? You really are amazing!

2 The human body is a **complex** machine. From the day we are born, our bodies grow and change in response to our environment, diet, and habits. The body has many different organ[2] systems and parts that work together to allow us to **breathe**, move, see, talk, and digest[3] food all at the same time. Most of the time we are unaware of what is happening in our bodies; usually it is only when we get sick or feel pain that we notice.

3 Many people do not take care of their complex machines. Bad habits like smoking, drinking too much alcohol, and eating junk food damage our bodies. Stress can also cause health problems. People who worry a lot or have busy jobs often don't get enough sleep, or don't eat properly. We can also damage our bodies when we play sports or get into accidents. Studies done by the Australian government show that most people get hurt because of an accidental slip or fall, or because of **injuries** from car accidents. It's true that a lot of people go to hospital because of serious **illnesses**, but far more people end up there because they simply weren't being careful.

4 Like machines, different body parts sometimes wear down from old age. People over the age of 65 are more likely to fall and hurt themselves, and these injuries—from bad cuts to broken bones—usually require serious medical attention. Due to the increase in the population of elderly people, gerontology is now one of the fastest-growing areas of medicine. There are many **treatments** available to help older people recover from illness and injury. It is now common for older people with damaged joints, for example, to have **surgery** to replace the old joint with a new one made of plastic or metal. Instead of **suffering** aches and pains through their retirement days, older people are able to lead happier and more comfortable lives.

5 As with any machine, the better you take care of it, the longer it will last. The best way to take care of your amazing machine is to eat the right foods, do regular exercise, and get enough sleep. Oh, and don't forget to smile!

---

[1] When you **frown**, you make an angry or unhappy expression with your face.
[2] An **organ** is a part of your body that has a special function, such as your heart or lungs.
[3] Your stomach **digests** food by breaking it down and taking what it needs for your body.

Reading Comprehension

Check Your Understanding

A **Choose the correct answers for the following questions.**

1 The writer lists facts about our body in paragraph 1 to _____.
   a show us how amazing our bodies are
   b test our knowledge about the body
   c remind us to take care of our body

2 Why does the writer say that we are *unaware of what is happening in our bodies* (line 13)?
   a We still don't know much about how our bodies work.
   b Our body works so smoothly that we don't notice it.
   c We don't really care about what happens in our body.

3 Doctors who study gerontology focus on _____.
   a doing research on the population of elderly people
   b creating technology for bones and joints
   c improving the health of older people

B **Circle the correct answer to complete each sentence.**

According to the passage . . .

1 Most people know (a lot / very little) about their bodies.
2 Most visits to the hospital are caused by (bad habits / accidents).
3 Our body is compared to a machine because it (is expensive to fix / has many complicated parts).
4 (Children / Old people) have the most accidents and health emergencies.

Critical Thinking

C **Discuss the following questions with a partner.**

1 The article talks about ways that our bodies are similar to machines. How are our bodies different from machines?
2 What advice would the writer give to readers who want to be healthier?

Vocabulary Comprehension

Words in Context

A **Choose the best answer. The words in blue are from the passage.**

1 Which is an example of an illness?
   a a broken leg   b a bad cold

2 What does surgery involve?
   a giving medicine   b cutting open a body

3 Which would make you suffer?
   a an injury   b a treatment

4 A cake consists of _____.
   a flour and eggs   b mixing and baking

5 Your body needs _____ to breathe.
   a air   b food

6 Which is an example of an injury from a car accident?

    a broken glass   **b** a broken leg

7 Which machine is more complex?

    a a computer   **b** a coffee maker

8 One treatment for a headache is _____.

    a resting   **b** listening to loud music

B **Answer the following questions, then discuss your answers with a partner. The words in blue are from the passage.**

1 Name a serious illness. What does it do to the body?

2 How long can you hold your breath?

3 What was the worst injury you've ever had? How did it happen?

4 Suggest a treatment for a stomachache.

A **Using a dictionary, match each root word with its meaning in the chart. Then combine the root word with the suffix *-logy/-ology* to complete the definitions.**

Vocabulary Skill
Nouns Ending in
-logy/-ology

Root Words	Meaning
bio •	• sound
psych •	• culture
phon •	• life
physio •	• nature/body
geo •	• mind
socio •	• earth

1 _____: the study of life

2 _____: the study of the mind

3 _____: the study of the earth

4 _____: the study of speech sounds

5 _____: the study of the body

6 _____: the study of culture

Learning the meanings of root words and suffixes can help you increase your vocabulary. In this chapter, you saw the word *gerontology*. The word is made up of the root word *geronto*, which means *old person*, and the suffix *-logy*, which means *the study of*.

B **Complete the following letter using words from A.**

Dear Aunt Marie,

How are you? My first year at the university is almost over and I haven't chosen my major yet! Mom wants me to be a doctor, so this semester, I took a **(1)** _____ class called "Introduction to Life Science" and a **(2)** _____ class called "The Human Mind." I didn't do very well, though, so maybe medicine isn't for me! I really enjoy reading *National Geographic* and learning about volanoes and earthquakes, so maybe I'll take a **(3)** _____ class next year. I'm coming home in three weeks—can't wait to see you!

Love, Judy

Motivational Tip: Set high expectations! Why are you studying English? Why is reading an important part of learning English? Five years from now, what do you hope to be doing in English? These questions can help you set higher expectations, or goals, for yourself.

ant

bat

eagle

dog

Before You Read
Stronger, Faster, Higher

A **Think about answers to the following questions.**

1 The animals above have special abilities. What do you think they are?

2 What do you think a human's special abilities are?

B **Discuss your answers with a partner.**

Reading Skill
Predicting Vocabulary

By thinking about the topic of a reading and the vocabulary that you expect to see, you can increase your understanding and your fluency in reading.

A **Look at the photo and the title of the passage on the next page. (Circle) the words that you expect to see in the passage.**

ability	cooking	phenomenon	blind	childhood
study	sight	deaf	body	dance
endurance	stress	memorize	school	nose
strain	determination	animals	eyes	
illness	athlete			

B **Read the passage to see if your answers in A were correct.**

C **Now read the entire passage carefully. Then answer the questions on page 66.**

Motivational Tip: What do others say about learning English? Have you read anything recently in a newspaper or a magazine about the importance of being a good reader? Who made the statement? Many influential people want to improve reading skills among people in their country. Do the leaders in your country have the same goals? How can you support those goals?

Seeing with the Ears

The human body is an amazing thing. People can train themselves to achieve unbelievable feats, from setting Olympic records to finding ways to **overcome** physical disabilities.[1] Ben
5 Underwood is a great example of someone who trained his body to do something incredible.

At the age of three, Ben went **blind** from retinal cancer, a type of eye cancer. When Ben
10 was about five years old, his mother noticed him making a clicking sound with his tongue that seemed to help him understand his surroundings. This skill, known as echolocation, is normally used by animals with very **sensitive** hearing, like dolphins and bats, for communication and to find food. They
15 make sounds and listen for the echo made when the sound waves hit an object and **bounce** back. Doctors tested Ben's hearing ability, but found it was normal. If Ben did not have superior hearing, how was he able to use echolocation?

Doctors used to believe blind people developed a sharper sense of hearing to help them overcome their loss of **sight**. Doctors did tests to try to confirm this, but just like in Ben's
20 case, the research showed that the test subjects generally had normal human hearing. It was through brain scans that doctors began to understand the **phenomenon** of echolocation. The scans show that when a blind person hears an echo, the parts of the brain that are related to vision are stimulated.

So even though blind people can't see with their eyes, their brains are able to determine
25 the shape and size of nearby objects. They move around an object, clicking and listening, to better understand its shape. This **refines** the picture of the object in their minds. In this way, blind people come to "see" their environment.

By the time he was a teenager, Ben Underwood could safely ride a bike and skateboard around his neighborhood using echolocation. Of course, it took Ben years of training his
30 mind and his senses to overcome his lack of sight. Sadly, Ben passed away in 2009 at the age of 16, but he remains a shining example of what people are **capable** of if they are determined enough.

---

[1] A **disability** is a permanent injury or illness that affects the way someone can live their life.

Reading Comprehension
Check Your Understanding

A Read the following sentences. Check (✔) true (*T*) or false (*F*).

		T	F
1	Ben was never able to see.		
2	Dolphins and bats make clicking sounds to know where to go.		
3	Doctors found that Ben had average hearing ability.		
4	Ben tried hard, but he was unable to ride a bike.		
5	A human brain can learn to analyze an echo.		

B Complete the following paragraph using words or phrases from the passage.

The human body really is amazing. **(1)** _____ was a teenager who showed us how people with **(2)** _____ can **(3)** _____ them. He went blind at a young age after getting **(4)** _____, yet he found a way to "see" his surroundings by making **(5)** _____. This is a skill called **(6)** _____ which is also used by dolphins and bats. Doctors once believed blind people developed **(7)** _____ to get around, which was proven to be untrue. Now they have learned using **(8)** _____ that the part of the brain that controls **(9)** _____ is stimulated when a blind person hears echoes. For Ben, learning to "see" took a long time, but it enabled him to cycle and **(10)** _____ around his neighborhood.

Critical Thinking

C Discuss the following questions with a partner.

1 What is the author's opinion about Ben Underwood? Give examples from the passage to support your answer.
2 How would learning how to use echolocation benefit a person who can see?

Vocabulary Comprehension
Definitions

A Match each word with its definition. The words in blue are from the passage.

1 _____ overcome   **a** unable to see
2 _____ blind   **b** a special or remarkable thing
3 _____ sensitive   **c** to make better
4 _____ bounce   **d** to hit an object and come back
5 _____ sight   **e** easily affected
6 _____ phenomenon   **f** able to do something
7 _____ refine   **g** the ability to see
8 _____ capable   **h** to succeed in dealing with a problem or difficulty

B **Complete the following sentences with the correct form of the words from A.**

1 You'll definitely be a better tennis player if you _____ your technique.
2 After weeks of practicing with friends, Kathy _____ her fear of speaking in front of a group.
3 Eagles use their powerful sense of _____ to find and catch prey.
4 Guide dogs are trained to lead _____ people around.
5 Marta wears sunglasses because her eyes are very _____ to light.
6 Lightning is a natural _____ that still cannot be fully exlained.
7 This car is _____ of speeds of up to 200 kilometers an hour.
8 Can you please stop _____ the ball? The sound is really annoying.

A **Look at the words below and complete the chart with the correct nouns. Use your dictionary if you need to.**

	Adjective/Verb	Noun
1	determined	*determination*
2	admire	_____
3	inspire	_____
4	compete	_____
5	distinct	_____
6	satisfy	_____

Vocabulary Skill
The Suffix *-ion*

In this chapter, you saw the noun *communication*. Many common nouns in English are formed by adding the suffix *-ion* to an adjective or verb.

B **Complete the paragraph below with the correct nouns from A.**

You might not have heard of Roger Bannister, but he has the **(1)** _____ of being the first person to run a mile (1.6 km) in under four minutes. He achieved this feat in 1954, during a **(2)** _____ between his running group and a team from Oxford University. At that time, people felt the "four minute barrier" could not be broken, and might even be physically dangerous. But Roger did not believe this, and trained with **(3)** _____ to achieve his goal. He finally ran a mile in 3 minutes and 59.4 seconds, earning the **(4)** _____ of runners worldwide. Roger later said that no matter how fast he got, he would only get **(5)** _____ from breaking the four-minute record. Even though the "four minute barrier" has been broken many times since, Roger's story still provides **(6)** _____ for athletes looking to run faster and better.

Real Life Skill

Finding the Right Doctor

Many people have a doctor they visit regularly. However, when a person has a serious illness or injury, or a special medical need, he or she will often visit a specialist. Learning the names of these types of doctors can help you identify the right health specialist.

A Study the list of root words in the chart. With a partner, discuss what the people whose names are listed below do.

Root	Meaning
derm-	skin
opt- / opthalmo-	eye
pod- / ped	foot
psych-	mind
dent-	teeth
gyn-	female

Dr. Kimberly Bentini, Dentist 555-2356

Dr. Martin Lewis, Podiatrist 555-9080

Dr. Sandy May, Gynecologist 555-2234

Dr. Peter Rodriguez, Dermatologist 555-0076

Dr. Mary Waters, Psychologist 555-6789

Dr. James Wong, Optometrist 555-8855

B You have the following problems. Using the page from the phone book above, write the phone number of the doctor you should call.

1 _____ You have a toothache.

2 _____ You can't read, so you need new glasses.

3 _____ Your sister is going to have a baby.

4 _____ You've been getting spots all over your face.

5 _____ You've been feeling really nervous and upset recently but you don't know why.

6 _____ The sides of your feet hurt when you run.

What do you think?

1 Why don't many people take good care of their bodies?

2 What more can you do to take better care of your health?

3 Do you think people are held back by their physical limitations or their mental limitations? Why?

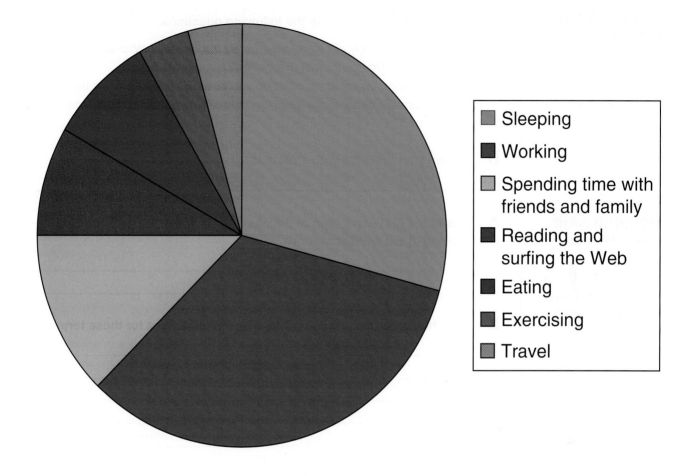

- ◼ Sleeping
- ◼ Working
- ◼ Spending time with friends and family
- ◼ Reading and surfing the Web
- ◼ Eating
- ◼ Exercising
- ◼ Travel

Getting Ready

Discuss the following questions with a partner.
1 Look at the pie chart above. Which activities involve leisure time?
2 What activities do you do in your leisure time?
3 How do you spend your day? Make a pie chart using your own information.

CHAPTER 1 Scrapbooking

Before You Read
Making Memories

A Think about the answers to the following questions.

1 Do you have many photos of your family and friends? Where do you keep them? Do you look at them often?
2 When you go on vacation, what do you keep to remember your trip?
3 Did your parents save any letters, documents, and photos from your childhood? Do you ever look at them?

B Discuss your answers with a partner.

Reading Skill
Finding Definitions

Sometimes a passage will give definitions or explanations of words that are related to the topic. The definitions may be shown by quotation marks "", parentheses ( ), or a dash —. When you find a new word, look carefully to see if the author has explained its meaning.

A Look at the first paragraph of the passage on the next page and find the meaning of the word *scrapbook*.

_____

_____

B Read the rest of the article and write the explanations for these terms.

layout:_____

_____

scrappers:_____

_____

LSS:_____

_____

C Read the entire passage carefully. Then answer the questions on page 72.

Motivational Tip: Are you a risk taker? Don't be afraid of making mistakes! Mistakes are a natural part of the learning process. Your classroom is the safest place in the world to study English and to make a mistake, so why not take a risk in this unit? What can you learn from making mistakes that will help you improve your reading?

Scrapbooking

The dictionary **defines** a scrapbook as "an empty book for collecting and **preserving** photographs, newspaper articles, and other papers." Today, *scrapbooking* is also a verb—and a popular new hobby. We talked with Diane Lucas, who runs a scrapbooking club.

What is scrapbooking exactly?
When I make a scrapbook page, I take a few of my family photos and put them into a "layout," which is a page that uses fancy paper, stickers, drawings, and words to show the theme. For example, I'm working on a page about my son called "First Day at School," so there's a photo of him and one of his drawings, and I **decorated** it with alphabet stickers. I use lots of things on my pages—ribbons, stickers, beads, and much more. When you make a scrapbook, you put words and pictures together to show the important times in your life. It's like a personal history.

How did you get started?
When I was a child, I always saved bits of paper. Things like movie tickets, vacation postcards, and even paper napkins. I loved looking at them and remembering. I made my first scrapbook ten years ago when my father died. When I looked through his desk, I found the most wonderful things—like my parents' anniversary cards and photos from his army days. I couldn't **throw away** anything, so I made two scrapbooks, one for my brother and one for me.

How do you learn about new scrapbooking techniques and trends?
The Internet is a great resource for new ideas. Many new "scrappers"—people who make scrapbooks—work from their computers, using digital photos and special software. But my favorite place to get new ideas is at scrapbooking trade shows. These shows feature new materials and techniques, offer workshops, and are a great way to meet people with the same interests.

Why is scrapbooking so popular these days?
I think people want to preserve their family history and **display** it for other people to see. When you make a scrapbook, you can pass the stories on to your children and your grandchildren. So many people today want to do that! In the U.S. alone, there are 2,500 LSS's (sorry; that's Local Scrapbooking Stores!) that sell paper and other **supplies** for scrapbooking. If you go online, you'll find scrapbooking websites from Norway, New Zealand, and South Africa. It's **universal**. We all have boxes of pictures and we all want to keep those **precious** memories. That's the real meaning of scrapbooking: sharing your family experiences and your story.

Reading Comprehension
Check Your Understanding

A Choose the correct answers for the following questions.

1 Which would you probably NOT put in a scrapbook?
   a pictures of your graduation ceremony
   b your household electricity bill
   c a poster of the concert that you performed in

2 When did Diane Lucas make her first scrapbook?
   a ten years ago, after her father died
   b on her parents' ten-year anniversary
   c on her son's first day at school

3 According to the last paragraph of the passage, which is true?
   a People prefer to buy scrapbooking supplies online.
   b Scrapbooking is more popular in South Africa than Norway.
   c People all over the world are taking an interest in scrapbooking.

B Read the following sentences. Check (✓) true (T) or false (F).

		T	F
1	A scrapbook page usually has a theme.		
2	People use a scrapbook to help them plan their future.		
3	People attend trade shows to learn new scrapbooking techniques.		
4	Most scrapbooks are about national history.		
5	Scrapbooking has become a big business worldwide.		

Critical Thinking

C Discuss the following questions with a partner.

1 What kinds of people do you think scrapbooking would be popular with?
2 Imagine you are going to make a scrapbook. What theme would you choose? What would you put in your scrapbook pages?

Vocabulary Comprehension
Odd Word Out

A Circle the word or phrase that does not belong in each group. The words in blue are from the passage.

1	preserve	keep	throw away	maintain
2	spoil	decorate	destroy	wreck
3	define	mistake	wrongdoing	error
4	show	display	assess	arrange

5	supplies	techniques	items	materials
6	worldwide	global	speaker	universal
7	useless	prized	precious	beloved

B Answer the following questions, then discuss your answers with a partner. The words in blue are from the passage.

1 What is something you would like to preserve for your children in the future?
2 When do you usually throw away a pair of shoes?
3 How do you like to decorate your room?
4 Do you think there will ever be a universal language?

A Create the noun form of the verbs below, then write a simple definition. Use your dictionary to help you. Discuss your answers with a partner.

Vocabulary Skill
The Suffix -ment

Many common nouns in English are formed by adding the suffix -ment to a verb, for example, enjoyment.

Verb	Noun	Meaning
improve	*improvement*	*making something better*
achieve		
measure		
develop		
require		
agree		
govern		

B Complete the following paragraph with either a verb or a noun from A.

A: It's quite a(n) **(1)** _____ to get into a university like Harvard or Yale.

B: Yes, I **(2)** _____ , but I'm not planning to attend either of those schools. I'm trying to enter Central University. The problem is that all international students have to take the TOEFL® test—it's a(n) **(3)** _____ .

A: Well, if you want to go there, you'll need to **(4)** _____ your test score.

B: I know, but my current score is still a(n) **(5)** _____ over last month's.

A: Well, I'm sure you'll get into Central—your English is very good. And you know that standardized tests don't always provide an accurate **(6)** _____ of a person's ability to speak in English.

C Now write three sentences of your own using the nouns from A.

1 _____
2 _____
3 _____

Before You Read
Leisure Survey

A Answer the following questions.

1 Rank the following kinds of entertainment from favorite (1) to least favorite (8).

_____ sitcoms	_____ dramas and soap operas
_____ movies	_____ talk shows
_____ news programs	_____ music videos
_____ nature and documentary shows	_____ video games

2 How many hours a day do you spend viewing the above? (Circle) the answer.

    0–1   2–3   4–5   6+

3 How do you usually access such entertainment? (Circle) the answer.

    on television   on a computer   other: _____

4 Complete this chart.

	Very true	Somewhat true	Not true at all
I like to watch shows alone.			
I like to watch shows with friends.			
I like to watch shows with family.			

B Discuss your answers with a partner.

Reading Skill
Recognizing Facts

It's important to know the difference between fact and opinion. A fact is always true. In contrast, opinions are signaled by *in my opinion*, *believe*, *think*, *might*, *may*, *probably*, *should*, *perhaps*, etc. Writers may also back up their opinions using facts, for example, *According to [survey name]...*

A Read the following sentences, then scan the passage to find information about each sentence. Check (✓) fact (**F**) or opinion (**O**).

		F	O
1	There are more movies and TV shows available online than on TV.		
2	The change from TV to Internet viewing is good.		
3	People pay more attention when they watch shows online.		
4	Not many people want to pay to watch shows online.		
5	The value of online entertainment has declined.		

B Now read the entire passage carefully. Then answer the questions on page 76.

Moving from TV to the Web

It used to be that if you wanted to watch a sitcom or a sporting event, you'd have to watch it from your television. As Internet technology improves, more and more shows
5 and movies are becoming available online. Broadcasting[1] companies are putting their primetime[2] shows directly on the Internet, and movie rental stores are **converting** their DVD collections to digital libraries.

10 This is probably a good change—at least for viewers. People can now pick exactly what they want to watch, and decide when and how they want to watch it. A study done by Harris Interactive found that more than half of Americans (56 percent) surf the Internet while "watching" television, and **approximately** 40 percent say that they read blogs or go on social networking sites at the same time. But this trend could be a problem for television
15 stations. Advertisers aren't getting a **response** from viewers, and they don't want to pay money if their commercials aren't being seen. In contrast, people who watch things online seem more engaged with what they watch. They read and write comments on the show, they look up **details** about the show, and they are less likely to ignore commercials. For broadcasters, online viewers may turn out to be more **loyal** fans.

20 Changing people's habits takes time. Even though many people are interested in watching television on the Internet, some may not want to make the **switch** completely. And some might be **persuaded** to, but only under certain circumstances. According to Harris, almost half of television viewers (44 percent) would cancel their cable television if they could get the same programs for free online. However, the number fell to 16 percent when people were told
25 they had to pay a small fee for online viewing. This is strange, since most households' monthly cable bills are the same or even more than what they would pay for the same shows online. It's possible that people have become so used to getting online entertainment for free that they learn not to value it as much.

Even with growing interest in online entertainment, people still think it is important to watch
30 television shows with their friends and family. People used to think that watching television would make families spend less time together, but it actually brought families closer for a few hours each night. Now it's feared that viewing shows online could make people more **isolated**. Who knows? Perhaps as online programming becomes more popular, people will find a way to make it into a social activity.

---

[1] A **broadcast** is a television program. Broadcasting companies create and sell these programs.
[2] **Primetime** is the time period when the most number of people are watching TV, usually between 6 pm and 10 pm on weekdays.

Reading Comprehension
Check Your Understanding

A Choose the correct answer for the following questions.

1 The writer puts quote marks around *watching* in line 13 to show viewers _____.

  a are not happy watching shows on television
  b are not paying attention to what they watch
  c would prefer to watch shows on the Internet

2 Which is NOT mentioned as proof that online viewers are more loyal?

  a They are willing to pay money to watch shows.
  b They watch the commercials during the show.
  c They want to find out more about the show.

3 What does the line *people have become so used to getting online entertainment for free that they learn not to value it as much* mean?

  a Online entertainment is becoming much more expensive.
  b The quality of online entertainment is not as good as on TV.
  c People feel they should not pay for something they used to get free.

B Read the following sentences. Check (✓) if they are true for television (*T*) or the Internet (*I*).

		T	I
1	People can choose to watch any show at any time.		
2	There is a growing potential for advertisers to make money.		
3	People are more willing to pay to watch shows.		
4	Viewers analyze and discuss the shows more.		
5	Families get together to watch shows at the end of the day.		

Critical Thinking

C Discuss the following questions with a partner.

1 Do you think technology isolates us, or brings us closer? Give examples.
2 Do you think people should pay for online entertainment? Why, or why not?

Vocabulary Comprehension
Words in Context

A Choose the best answer. The words in blue are from the passage.

1 When you convert something, you _____ it.
  a get rid of   b change

2 You use an approximate number when you _____ the actual number.
  a know   b don't know

3 A response comes _____ an event.
  a after   b before

4 The _____ in a passage contains details.

   a heading   **b** paragraph

5 My dog is very loyal; he _____ walks beside me.

   a never   **b** always

6 You switch to something else if you _____ the first thing.

   a like   **b** don't like

7 A _____ needs to be able to persuade people.

   a police officer   **b** salesperson

8 If you feel isolated, then you feel _____ .

   a alone   **b** hungry

B **Answer the following questions, then discuss your answers with a partner. The words in blue are from the passage.**

   1 Approximately how many foreign countries have you been to?

   2 How would you respond to someone who was rude to you?

   3 Which brands are you most loyal to? What would persuade you to switch to a different brand?

A **For each word in the box below, complete the associations using the vocabulary shown. Then explain to a partner how the words in each group are related. Can you add more words to these associations?**

> commuting   hobby   email   common   download   enjoy   hectic

   1 activity: _____   pastime

   2 computer: _____   _____

   3 workweek: _____   work

   4 leisure: relax   _____

   5 pressure: _____   stress

   6 popular: _____   frequent

B **Use the "starter" words below to create word associations of your own. Begin by saying the word to a partner. Your partner should reply with a word that is related. Continue until you have a six-word association. Share your answers with the class.**

   Example: food: *delicious, pizza, Italy, spaghetti, tomatoes, garden*

   1 relax: _____ , _____ , _____ ,

       _____ , _____ , _____ .

   2 travel: _____ , _____ , _____ ,

       _____ , _____ , _____ .

   3 school: _____ , _____ , _____ ,

       _____ , _____ , _____ .

   4 (your own idea) Word: _____ Associations: _____ ,

       _____ , _____ , _____ .

       _____ , _____ .

Vocabulary Skill
Word Associations

In learning new vocabulary, think about how words are related, or associated, with other words. Think about words with similar meanings, for example *hobby* and *activity*. Also think about words that are related to the same topic, e.g. *scissors* and *paper*.

Real Life Skill
Using Key Words for Internet Searches

Before you begin to search for information on the Internet, ask yourself, "What am I looking for?" To find information about a specific topic (e.g. the origin of pop music), you should use key nouns, verbs, and adjectives. Think of some key word synonyms that might also help you find information about your topic.

A You have to do some Internet research for an essay with the topic *The Origins of Pop Music*. Can you think of more key words you can use?

Key words: *origins, beginning, pop music, pop songs*

B Look at the following topics. (Circle) the key words you would use for your Internet research. Then write other words which would be useful. Compare your ideas with a partner.

1 learning how to use a digital camera to take photographs
Other words: _____

2 keeping tropical fish in an aquarium at home
Other words: _____

3 simple recipes for beginners to learn cooking
Other words: _____

4 biographies of film actors and actresses
Other words: _____

C Choose one topic from **B** and do an Internet search using your key words. Share any useful websites you find with your classmates.

Topic: _____

Sites that were useful: _____

_____

_____

Can the information on a website be trusted? Remember to ask yourself:

- Who wrote the information? How experienced are they in the topic?
- Are there many facts, or is the information mostly the writer's opinion?
- When was the information written? Is it up-to-date?
- Does the website provide links to other useful websites?

Motivational Tip: How can this be applied beyond the textbook? Reading is a very important life skill and is used every day to accomplish real life tasks. How can the real life skill of doing research on the Internet be used in everyday life?

What do you think?

1 How has modern technology changed the way people spend their leisure time?
2 Do people in your country have enough time for leisure? Why, or why not?
3 What leisure activities are popular with young people in your country? Which are more popular with older people?

Fluency Strategy: PQR+E

Parsing, **Q**uestioning, **R**ephrasing, and **E**xplaining (PQR+E) is a reading strategy to help you build your reading comprehension in stages from sentences to paragraphs to full texts. Use this strategy when you have difficulty understanding large pieces of text that you are reading.

Parsing

The first step in PQR+E is **parsing**—breaking a sentence into smaller parts. When you come to sentences that are long or difficult to understand, try parsing them into smaller pieces.

A **Look at one way the first sentence in the passage on the next page, *Movies for the Blind*, can be broken into smaller parts. Doing this can make it much easier to work out the overall meaning of the sentence.**

> When you think of the cinema, the phrase *watching a movie* probably comes to mind, and, indeed, moviemakers work very hard to make their films interesting visually.

When you think / of the cinema, / the phrase watching a movie / *probably / comes to mind, / and, indeed, / moviemakers work very hard / to make their films / interesting visually.*

B **Now look at another sentence of the passage. Parse this sentence by dividing it into smaller parts.**

> Movies also contain dialogue, music, and sound effects—things that people don't need to see in order to enjoy.

Questioning

The second step in PQR+E is **questioning**. Once you have finished parsing a long sentence, ask yourself questions about the parts of the sentence. What do you understand? What do you not understand?

Review the first two sentences from *Movies for the Blind*. What questions do you have as you read them? Read the example question for the first sentence, then write your own for the second sentence.

1   How are movies interesting, besides visually?

2   _____

Rephrasing

In step 3 of PQR+E, **rephrasing**, write in your own words what the sentence you parsed means. Rephrasing helps you show that you have understood what you have read.

Read the example paraphrase of the first sentence of *Movies for the Blind*. Then write in your own words what the other sentence means to you.

1 When people think about movies, they mostly think about the visual features.
   The visual features of movies are also very important to filmmakers.

2 _____

Explaining (or Extending)

In the final step of PQR+E you **explain** what you have understood to a partner. Explaining what you understand to someone else helps strengthen your comprehension.

A **Explain the meaning of the two example sentences from *Movies for the Blind* to a partner.**

B **Use PQR+E as you continue reading the passage, especially if there is a sentence you do not understand.**

Movies for the Blind

When you think of the cinema, the phrase *watching a movie* probably comes to mind, and, indeed, moviemakers work very hard to make their films interesting visually. They may use elaborate costumes, beautiful locations, or amazing special effects to tell a story. An actor's expression or movements can also sometimes say more than words.

But what about people who are blind or have trouble seeing? Movies also contain dialogue, music, and sound effects—things that people don't need to see in order to enjoy. Movie reviewer Marty Klein, who is blind, created a website called Blindspots to help people choose movies that they can follow without the help of someone explaining what is happening on the screen. He gave a rating, from 1 to 10, based on several things. A movie received a high rating if it has only a few main characters whose voices are easy to recognize. Klein also liked interesting stories without too many changes in time and place. A large amount of dialogue between the characters was better than long silences or noisy action scenes. His reviews are still online, but the site is no longer updated.

Another blind movie reviewer, Jay Forry, maintains the website Blindside Reviews. He also writes for newspapers and is a guest on radio shows. Forry gives movies one of five ratings, including, "So good, blind people like it" and "I'm glad I couldn't see it." Forry became a writer after going blind at the age of 28, and his writing skills and sense of humor are what keep people reading his reviews or listening to him on the radio. After "watching" the animated movie *Up*, Forry commented that he wished he, too, could have a talking dog to tell him to watch out for cars and to not "go into the ladies' restroom again."

Sometimes, though, it's nice to go to a movie without reading reviews and knowing what to expect. Some movie theaters have begun to offer recorded audio descriptions of the movements, scenery, and special effects so that blind moviegoers can follow what other audience members see on the screen. They usually receive a wireless headset to wear during the movie. This allows them to listen to the narration while still hearing the movie's music and other sounds that surround them in the theater. Jay Forry also notes that modern theaters now have excellent sound systems, something he appreciates more than the average moviegoer.

In the end, going to the movies should be a fun and exciting experience—for both the sighted and the blind.

C Answer the following comprehension questions.

1 What is the main idea of the article?
  a Jay Forry writes movie reviews for blind people.
  b Blind people have resources to help them enjoy movies.
  c Some movie reviews are written specifically for blind people.
  d Blind people do not enjoy going to movies.

2 Which movie would probably receive the best rating from Marty Klein?
  a a foreign martial arts film with many fight scenes
  b a drama that often shifts between the past and the present
  c a romantic comedy with four main characters and lots of conversation
  d a space adventure with many explosions and special effects

3 Movie reviewer Jay Forry has his own _____ .
  a website
  b newspaper
  c radio show
  d movie theater

4 What is Jay Forry most likely to say about a movie he dislikes?
  a He wishes it hadn't been made.
  b It might have been good if he could see.
  c He is very happy he is blind.
  d Other blind people might like it.

5 Why does the author include this quotation: "go into the ladies' restroom again"?
  a to recommend the movie *Up* to readers
  b to compare Forry to the dog in the movie *Up*
  c to illustrate Forry's sense of humor
  d to demonstrate Forry's need for help

6 To help blind people, some theaters _____ .
  a offer special headsets that play a recorded description of the movie
  b hold events for blind people to see movies together
  c give a discount on movie tickets to blind people
  d provide people to sit next to blind people and describe the movie

7 What does line 46–47 *something he appreciates...average moviegoer* mean?
  a Jay Forry is a better movie critic than most people in the audience.
  b Jay Forry needs to test if wireless headsets help blind people.
  c Jay Forry needs to pay attention to sound so he can write a movie review.
  d Jay Forry pays more attention to sound.

SELF CHECK

Answer the following questions.

1 Have you ever used the PQR+E method before?

☐ Yes ☐ No ☐ I'm not sure.

2 Will you practice PQR+E in your reading outside of English class?

☐ Yes ☐ No ☐ I'm not sure.

3 Do you think PQR+E is helpful? Why, or why not?

_____

_____

4 When you are reading, do you find yourself having to translate? If yes, what do you think you can do to stop translating?

_____

_____

5 Which of the six reading passages in units 4–6 was easiest? Which was most difficult? Why?

_____

_____

6 What have you read in English outside of class recently?

_____

_____

7 What improvements are you making as a reader? Look again at the *Tips for Fluent Reading* on pages 8 and 9. Write down one or two things that you know you can do better today than when you started the course.

_____

_____

8 What other improvements do you still want to make as a reader?

_____

_____

Fluency Practice

Time yourself as you read through the passage. Try to read as fluently as you can. Record your time in the Reading Rate Chart on page 176. Then answer the questions on page 85.

Raising a Child Athlete

1 In many countries, children with sporting potential are identified early and encouraged to achieve athletic greatness by training for hours every day. While some people see this as a great opportunity for kids to be healthy, others argue that too much focus on training can hurt young people. How parents should raise child athletes has become a big topic of their debate.

2 5 People who are against such serious commitment to sports say that there are many negatives to training so intensely. Here are some of their arguments:

- The long hours spent training can distance the child from his or her family.
- Athletes who spend too much time training miss out on education. The child may not be prepared for other real world activities, such as going to college and having a
10 non-athletic job.
- Pressure from parents and coaches to win can be psychologically damaging for the child. Parents may also become too pushy and end up caring more about athletic achievements than the child.

3 Dr. Christine Carr, a psychologist, suggests that parents take some important steps to make
15 sure that their kids are getting the most out of sports. Carr says that the focus should be on the child's happiness and about learning life lessons. Self-discipline, determination, and learning to deal with failure are some of the important life skills and lessons kids can learn from sports.

4 Other experts point to the importance of letting children make their own decisions. Top athletes Tiger Woods and Michael Phelps have said that they
20 appreciated their parents letting them decide how much or how little they wanted to train. In fact, according to Phelps' mother, he had trouble focusing in the classroom until he found a sport that he was passionate about. By allowing Michael to focus on his sport, his mother also saw him improve as a student.

5 25 Another thing that many parents and doctors agree on is the importance of developing a close relationship with the family. Dr. Carr suggests eating dinner together and says it is a simple way to remind children that family is important, and that support can always be found at home. Woods and Phelps both had supportive families and
30 made it public, with parents attending their many competitions.

Michael Phelps and his mother Debbie

6 Raising an athlete is not easy. By balancing life and training, parents can set their children up for success and help them become winners in sports and in life.

398 words   **Time taken** _____

Reading Comprehension

1 What is this passage mainly about?
  a why training child athletes is wrong
  b when child athletes should begin training
  c how parents can decide if their child would make a good athlete
  d how parents can raise child athletes the right way

2 The purpose of the second paragraph is to ____ .
  a examine what child psychologists say
  b list arguments against training young athletes
  c compare arguments for and against training young athletes
  d list bad ways to train children

3 What best describes Dr. Carr's opinion of children in sports?
  a She thinks sports have the potential to benefit children.
  b She is against children playing sports.
  c She thinks only teenagers should play sports.
  d She thinks sports are good but meaningless for children.

4 What is said about failure in the third paragraph?
  a It should be avoided.
  b It happens when athletes don't train hard enough.
  c It is something child athletes should not think about.
  d It is something children should learn to deal with.

5 Why does the writer use Tiger Woods and Michael Phelps as examples?
  a They are very rich and successful athletes.
  b They had supportive families as child athletes.
  c They have spoken about the dangers of training too hard.
  d They are now raising their children as child athletes.

6 Why does Dr. Carr say families should eat dinner together at home?
  a because it is an important meal for child athletes
  b because otherwise the children might eat fast food
  c because children should spend their evenings at home
  d because it teaches children the importance of family

7 Who would find this passage the most useful?
  a child psychologists
  b coaches of child athletes
  c parents of child athletes
  d adult athletes

The Life of a Professional Gamer

Gordon Hayward has a pretty cool job—he plays basketball for the team Utah Jazz in the American National Basketball Association (NBA). But in his free time, he also works as a professional gamer, competing in *Starcraft 2* tournaments. Even
5 as a top-level athlete, Gordon is impressed with the amount of commitment needed for these competitions. "These guys are professionals," he says. "They play this game for their job, so they take this as seriously as I take playing basketball for a living."

Competitive gaming has been around for almost as long as video
10 games themselves, but it's only recently that people have started earning money from it. This is because companies sponsor[1] gamers and tournaments. The gaming industry is now worth about $6 billion, and it is growing every year. Michel Masquelier, President of IMG Media (one of the world's largest entertainment companies), called gaming the number one activity in the world for men aged 18 to 24. Just as young people aspire to play in the NBA, many also dream of becoming
15 professional gamers.

There are now big global tournaments like World Cyber Games and Major League Gaming Championships, where hundreds of gamers come to compete in popular games like *Starcraft, Warcraft, Counterstrike*, and the football game *FIFA* in front of an audience. The prize money in a tournament can reach a few million dollars.

20 One thing gamers and athletes have in common is that they often play in teams. These "clans," as gamers call them, usually play tournaments together and practice against one another. Professional gamers and their clans earn money through sponsorships, winning tournaments, and teaching and training people to play video games better.

Like athletes, gamers must train long and hard to become the best at the games that they play.
25 Most gamers only compete in one game, the same way that most professional athletes only play one sport. Adrian Kwong, a professional gamer, says that he usually practices *Starcraft 2* for more than three hours. Some days he even plays for more than five hours! "To become a pro player, it takes determination, skill, and extensive practice," says Katie Goldberg, who is vice-president of communications at Major League Gaming.

30 Gordon Hayward isn't going to give up his basketball career anytime soon, but he says that athletes and gamers are not that different: "You have to train hard if you want to be the best, and that goes for everything, not just basketball. That also goes for video games like *Starcraft*."

---

[1]A person or organization **sponsors** an activity or event by paying for it to happen, normally so they can advertise a product.

416 words   **Time taken** _____

Reading Comprehension

1 What best describes the main idea of the passage?
    a While popular, video game sports are not real sports.
    b Professional gamers earn as much as athletes.
    c Professional gamers train and compete like athletes.
    d More athletes are playing video games than ever before.

2 Why does the writer say in lines 4–5 that Gordon is impressed *even as a top-level athlete*?
    a Athletes are used to training long and hard.
    b Ahletes generally don't like playing video games.
    c Athletes don't have time to play video games.
    d Athletes enter lots of competitions as well.

3 Why does the passage say gamers have recently started earning money?
    a Competitive gaming is very new.
    b Gamers now work for video game companies.
    c Young people pay to watch their favorite gamers.
    d Companies now sponsor gamers and competitions.

4 What is a "clan"?
    a a club for fans of gamers
    b a team of gamers
    c a person who is new to gaming
    d a gamer who no longer competes

5 Which is true about gaming tournaments?
    a Only the top gamers compete.
    b Gamers play from their homes.
    c Winners receive trophies, but not money.
    d Fans watch gamers as they play.

6 Professional gamers like Adrian Kwong _____ .
    a do some physical exercise to help their gaming
    b take part in gaming competitions on their own
    c practice for many hours a day
    d compete in many different games

7 The purpose of the final paragraph is to show _____ .
    a how athletes and gamers are the same
    b how athletes and gamers are different
    c why Gordon Hayward plays video games like *Starcraft 2*
    d why Gordon Hayward chooses basketball over video games

Friday

- Sandor Nagy and the National Orchestra present an evening of Beethoven's classics. Festival Hall, 8 p.m.
- DJ 2-Cool from Los Angeles (with special guests) plays the latest dance hits. The Warehouse, from 10 p.m.

Saturday

- Save the planet! Ten top bands play all night at *Rock & Roll for the World*, a benefit concert for environmental groups. Riverside Theater, from 6 p.m.
- Hear the Jazz All-Stars—five of the greatest names in jazz, together for the first time. Lacey's Lounge, 9 p.m.
- Join us at Salsa Fest, with BIG prizes for the best dancers! Club Tropicale, from 9 p.m.

Sunday

- From Jamaica—hear reggae band One Love in concert. Metro Auditorium, 8 p.m.
- Join the Ireland Festival for real Irish food and drink, and some great tunes. Cross-Cultural Center, from 4 p.m. until late.

Getting Ready

Read the event flyer above, then discuss the following questions with a partner.
1 What kind of music would you hear at each event?
2 Which event would you like to go to? Why?

Before You Read
My Favorite Music

A Look at the different styles, or genres, of music below. Which ones have you heard of? (Circle) the ones you like. ~~Cross out~~ the ones you don't like.

rock	classical	folk	reggae
blues	country	jazz	hip-hop/rap
house/techno	pop	salsa	_____

B Discuss your answers with a partner. How many other genres of music can you name?

Reading Skill
Predicting

> Before you read, it's helpful to review what you already know about the topic. This will help you to predict the things you will read about, and will increase your understanding of the reading.

A (Circle) the words or phrases which best complete the following sentences. Can you predict what the passage on the next page will be about?

1 Traditional music is found in (many / only a few) countries in the world.
2 To keep traditional music alive, young people need to (learn music from / teach music to) older people.
3 Researchers think music is an (important / unimportant) party of history.
4 Researchers are trying to record older, traditional music so that it (doesn't disappear / becomes more popular).
5 If you are listening to a field recording, you are listening to musicians performing in a (studio / natural setting).

B Scan the passage on the next page to see if your answers in **A** were correct.

C Now read the entire passage carefully. Then answer the questions on page 90.

Motivational Tip: Sucess or failure? Effort or ability? When you suceed, is it because of your effort or your ability? Sucess can be a combination of both, but effort is perhaps more important. When you suceed, remember that it is because of the time you spent working on it. When you fail, remember it is not because you are not good enough, but because you need to spend more time and energy on the task.

Sounds from the Past

Much of the music we listen to today is a mixture of styles from various countries and time periods. A lot of music has **roots** in older traditional songs heard in many different countries around the world. Traditional, or folk, music is collected over decades, if not centuries. Younger generations
5 learn these songs from their elders through practice and repetition.

Since music can tell us a lot about different cultures through its **lyrics**, melodies, and the instruments used, researchers and music fans see it as an **essential** part of history. They fear that traditional and older types of music are slowly disappearing, partly because they are less likely to
10 be written down or recorded, or because the **format** in which they are recorded is no longer in use. Also, younger generations may not find such music very **appealing**, so once older generations pass away, the music may die out with them. Whole genres of music may go **extinct**.

People play bamboo flutes with their noses.

There is a growing effort to preserve music in its many forms. Some
15 researchers create field recordings—recordings made outside of a recording studio—to **capture** live performances. For example, in the early 1900s, social scientist Frances Densmore made recordings of Native American songs that had been sung for many generations but were in danger of being forgotten. Researchers also transcribe old music by listening to old recordings—sometimes the only one of its kind left. They try to write out the music
20 so that it can be studied and played by modern musicians.

Collecting music is another form of music preservation. Some collectors are extremely passionate about their music, and will spend a lot of time and money looking for things that have not been produced or sold for many years. Their efforts help to document music of different cultures, **genres**, time periods, and places. For example, some punk rock fans still collect cassette tapes from the 70s, while many jazz fans prefer to listen to old vinyl records.

Folk musicians from the island of Madagascar

There are also associations and societies to preserve and celebrate very specific kinds of music. For example, the Idelsohn Society helps to preserve old and rare Jewish music, the Suni Project celebrates
30 the work of Grikor Marzaian Suni, an old and influential Armenian composer, while the Videogame Music Preservation Foundation lets people listen to old videogame music in its original form.

Now, modern technology makes it much easier to preserve music.
35 Smartphones can be used to record music, while the Internet lets us share these recordings and find people with similar interests. Soon, losing a piece of music may be a thing of the past.

Reading Comprehension
Check Your Understanding

A Check (✓) the statements that you think the author would agree with.

1 ☐ Young people are less likely to care about traditional songs and music than older people.
2 ☐ People like Frances Densmore have worked hard to save traditional music.
3 ☐ Music researchers and music collectors are actually quite similar in what they do.
4 ☐ Modern musicians can learn from traditional music.
5 ☐ The Internet and smartphones have the potential to help save traditional music.

B Choose the correct answers for the following sentences.

According to the article . . .
1 Traditional music is collected over _____ years.
  a many   **b** a few
2 Researchers sometimes have _____ recordings of the music they are studying.
  a many   **b** very few
3 The purpose of associations like the Suni Project is to _____ .
  a celebrate traditional music   **b** plan music events
4 Field recordings are recorded _____ a studio.
  a in   **b** outside
5 Transcribing music requires _____ music.
  a listening to and writing   **b** recording live

Critical Thinking

C Discuss the following questions with a partner.

1 What kinds of traditional music have you heard? Which country or area was it from?
2 Can you think of more ways to help preserve traditional music?

Vocabulary Comprehension
Definitions

A Match each word with its definition. The words in blue are from the passage.

1	_____ roots	**a**	type or style of music, art, or literature
2	_____ extinct	**b**	the way in which something is presented
3	_____ lyrics	**c**	having ended or died out
4	_____ format	**d**	to represent or record in order to preserve it
5	_____ appealing	**e**	the origins of something or someone
6	_____ capture	**f**	the words of a song
7	_____ genre	**g**	necessary, very important
8	_____ essential	**h**	interesting or attractive

B Complete the following sentences with the correct form of the words from **A**.

1 The music from the 1960s, such as the Beatles and Jimi Hendrix, is still _____ to young people today.

2 The _____ of rock and roll has its _____ in other music types: it's a style of music that developed from rhythm and blues, gospel, jazz, and country music.

3 In a karaoke booth, the _____ to the songs are usually shown on a TV screen.

4 Jeff feels that listening to a musician playing live is a(n) _____ part of the musical experience.

A Read the passage below, and circle all of the *ex-* words you find.

Tokyo Concert Review

Last night was the first Asian concert of rock band Small Minds' world tour. The band began their exhausting tour six months ago in New York. They are so popular in the States that they extended their stay there by a week, and played five extra concerts that sold out within hours.

In an interview before their concert yesterday, guitarist Lee Gray and lead singer Mark Lang said they were very excited to be in Tokyo. "This is our first trip to Japan, so it's a fantastic experience for us," said Lang.

The extensive tour continues to Nagoya, Osaka, and Fukuoka before moving to Korea, China, Thailand, Malaysia, Singapore, and the Philippines. Small Minds then plan to take a hard-earned break at an exclusive island resort before heading back home to the U.K. From there they will start the European leg of the tour. If you're lucky enough to get tickets to see them, expect a loud and energetic show, with some fantastic new versions of their album songs.

Vocabulary Skill
The Prefix *ex-*

In this chapter, you read the adjective *extinct*, which means to *die out completely*. *Ex-* comes at the beginning of many words to form nouns, verbs, adjectives, and adverbs in English. It means *upwards*, *completely*, *without*, and *former*.

B Match each of the *ex-* words from **A** with the definitions below.

1 _____: limited or restricted to certain groups or people

2 _____: very tiring

3 _____: feeling happy and thrilled

4 _____: great or large in size, length

5 _____: made something longer in space or time

6 _____: more than usual; additional

7 _____: an event or happening

C Are there other words that begin with *ex-* that you can add to this list? What do they mean? Share your ideas with a partner.

Before You Read
My Music

A **Answer the following questions.**

1 Do you have a favorite musician? Why do you like him or her?
2 How do you get information about new music? (e.g., through friends, music websites, magazines, etc.)
3 How do you decide which music to buy?

B **Discuss your answers with a partner.**

Reading Skill
Noticing Patterns

Before reading a passage, we look at the format of the article and scan it for patterns. Examining how an article is set up helps you read more quickly and find important information easily.

A **Skim the reviews on the next page and answer the following questions.**

1 How many albums are reviewed?
2 Which album was released earliest?
3 How many albums play for longer than one hour?

B **The information below can be found in the album reviews on the next page. Scan the reviews, then number the information from 1–6 as it appears.**

_____ the date the album was released
___1___ the name of the musician or band
_____ the length of the album
_____ summary of the writer's opinion
_____ the writer's opinion of the album
_____ the name of the album

C **Now read the reviews carefully. Then answer the questions on page 94.**

Motivational Tip: Share with others. Think of two ways to share what you learn from this chapter with people who are not in your class. Do you have a friend that you could send an email to after class? Tell him or her about the importance of preserving traditional music, or share information about an album you just discovered. As you share what you read with others, your reading skills will improve.

For the Record: Album Reviews

In this month's *For the Record*, we review a selection of classic records that created a **revolution** in the music world. Each of these records appeared in the top 10 of *Rolling Stone* magazine's 500 greatest albums of all time.

The Beach Boys – *Pet Sounds* (1966)
Length 35:57

5   When The Beach Boys **released** *Pet Sounds*, they were already famous for their all-American image and California-style "surf rock" sound. However, *Pet Sounds* showed how the band had grown stronger and more **mature** in their music. Not only did
10   they use more instruments than usual, they used a variety of sounds such as dog barks and trains to create their music. The **album** features the hit songs "Wouldn't It Be Nice" and "God Only Knows," and inspired another great album—The Beatles'
15   *Sgt. Pepper's Lonely Hearts Club Band*.
In short: This is a great record for both fans and general listeners.

Bob Dylan – *Highway 61 Revisited* (1965)
Length 51:26

20   In his early career, Bob Dylan was considered a folk music hero. He was known for his live shows, playing the acoustic guitar,[3] and singing songs about everyday life. Named for the road he grew up on, *Highway 61 Revisited* is very different from Dylan's
25   earlier sound. On the record, Dylan plays an electric guitar and sings songs about politics and culture in America in the 1960s. Many fans were shocked by this change, but the record affected the course of music forever.
30   *In short:* Buy this classic album for Dylan's poetic lyrics.

Marvin Gaye – *What's Going On* (1971)
Length 35:38

In the late 1960s, American soul singer Marvin Gaye saw many problems around him— war, poverty[1], homelessness, the negative effects of drug use—and felt the need to make a **statement**. *What's Going On* is written from the perspective of a war veteran,[2] and the songs comment on social problems in a way that soul music never had before. Gaye's record company was sure the record—his 11th—would fail, but the title track was very successful, and so was the record. *What's Going On* was the first of many soul records to take on social issues.
In short: This is an important record for any music fan. Focus your attention on the lyrics to really understand the music.

The Clash – *London Calling* (1979)
Length 65:07

Punk **pioneers** The Clash crossed many music **boundaries** with their third album, *London Calling*. While the band kept their original punk sound, these songs also **incorporate** bits of jazz, ska, reggae, pop, and soul. The Clash were known for expressing their political views through their music, and *London Calling* comments on many problems in Britain at that time. This album showed that punk can and should be taken seriously.
In short: This album is a great introduction to punk rock, but for true fans, spend your money on the rare live-music recordings.

---

[1] Someone living in **poverty** is very poor.
[2] A **veteran** is someone who has fought in a war.
[3] An **acoustic guitar** is a traditional guitar that doesn't use electricity.

Reading Comprehension
Check Your Understanding

A Read the following sentences. Check (✓) true (*T*) or false (*F*).

		T	F
1	The four records are said to be very important in music history.		
2	The Beach Boys sound more mature in their album *Pet Sounds*.		
3	Marvin Gaye inspired the Beatles to make an album.		
4	*Highway 61 Revisited* is named for the store where Bob Dylan bought his guitar.		
5	The Clash released two albums before *London Calling*.		

B Read the following sentences. Which album(s) do the sentences describe? Check (✓) Pet Sounds (*P*), What's Going On (*W*), Highway 61 Revisited (*H*), or London Calling (*L*).

		P	W	H	L
1	This album talks about social and political issues.				
2	A wide variety of instruments were used on this album.				
3	Fans are told to get the live recordings of this album's songs instead.				
4	The artist was already famous before this album was released.				
5	This album was released by a British band/musician.				

Critical Thinking

C Discuss the following questions with a partner.

1 Which of the albums have you listened to? Which would you like to listen to most? Why?

2 What other albums do you think have changed music? Why?

Vocabulary Comprehension
Words in Context

A Choose the best answer. The words in blue are from the passage.

1 If something is a revolution, it changes people's ideas _____ .
   a quickly   **b** slowly

2 When a book is released, who is able to see it?
   a the public   **b** the writer

3 Mature people usually have _____ experience.
   a less   **b** more

4 Who is likely to create an album?

    a a writer   **b** a musician

5 Which is an example of statement?

    a Is that the right thing to do?   **b** What you are doing is wrong.

6 The Misfits and The Ramones were pioneers of punk music. In other words, they came _____ in the movement.

    a early   **b** later

7 A fence creates a boundary _____ a home.

    a around   **b** within

8 If you incorporate A into B, you _____.

    a add A to B   **b** replace A with B

B **Answer the following questions, then discuss your answers with a partner. The words in blue are from the passage.**

1 How can you tell when someone is mature? What qualities do they have?

2 Do you think it is important for music to make a statement? Why, or why not?

3 How can you incorporate the skills for learning a language into other parts of your life?

A **Compare the noun *effect* and the verb *affect*. Use each in a sentence below.**

> **effect** /ɪˈfect/ *n.* a change that is caused by something or is the result of something
> **affect** /əˈfect/ *v.* to do something that changes someone or something

1 This book really _____ how I think about relationships.

2 This book had a great _____ on me; I think about relationships much differently now.

B **Look at the word pairs below. Choose the correct word for the following sentences. Use a dictionary to help you.**

1 Marta gave me some good (advice / advise) for my trip to Spain.

2 If you visit Madrid, I would (advice / advise) you to stay in a guesthouse near the Retiro Park.

3 Everyone (accept / except) Paul is going to the concert on Friday night.

4 Ben, this is a lovely gift, but I can't (accept / except) it. It's too expensive!

5 Graciela is older (then / than) Lucia.

6 I'm free at 8:00. Can we meet (then / than)?

7 Smoking and drinking too much can (effect / affect) your health in a negative way.

8 Smoking and drinking too much can have a negative (effect / affect) on your health.

Vocabulary Skill
Easily Confused Words

In this unit, you've seen the words *effect* and *affect*. Words like this are often confused because they are spelled in a similar way, and in spoken English, are sometimes pronounced alike.

Real Life Skill
Dictionary Usage
Choosing the Right Word

In English, there are many words that are similar in meaning but are not exactly the same. A good English dictionary has examples that show how each word is used. These examples can help you choose the correct word.

A *Expect, hope,* and *look forward to* are similar in meaning. Read the dictionary entries below, then complete the following sentences. Explain your choices to a partner.

expect *v.* to believe very strongly that something will happen
Example: *I expect it to be sunny tomorrow, since the weather forecast says there will be good weather for the rest of the week.*

hope *v.* to want something to happen, to believe that there is a possibility that it can happen
Example: *I hope it will be sunny tomorrow as I really want to go to the beach.*

look forward to *phr. v.* to expect that something will happen and to be very excited about it; to anticipate something
Example: *I look forward to going to the beach tomorrow with my friends.*

1 The audience has paid a lot of money for this show, so they _____ it to be entertaining.

2 I'm really _____ a two-week vacation; it'll be great to have some time away from school!

3 I would love to get a new TV. I _____ to buy one next year if I can save enough money.

4 I studied really hard for this exam, so I at least _____ to pass.

B Now write a sentence each for *expect, hope,* and *look forward to.* Share your sentences with a partner.

1 _____

2 _____

3 _____

What do you think?

1 Have musical styles from other countries influenced the music scene in your country? Give some examples.

2 Who are the most popular musicians in your country right now? Do you like them? Do you know of any musicians in your country who sing in another language?

3 Do you know any song lyrics in English? Say or sing a song for your partner!

Career Paths

1950s

Telegraph Operator: People sent and received telegrams, which were messages sent using Morse Code through underground and undersea cables.

1970s

Typists: Women worked in "typist pools" where they typed letters and forms for managers in an office.

1920s

Cow Milkers: People milked every cow on the farm twice a day by hand.

Getting Ready

Discuss these questions with a partner.

1 Why are the jobs above no longer needed? What jobs have they been replaced with?
2 Which jobs today do you think will no longer be needed in 20 years? Why?

CHAPTER 1 College Start-Ups

Before You Read
Would You Start a Business?

A **Think about answers to the following questions.**

1   A "start-up" is a very small business that is still in the process of growing. Would you like to have a start-up? Why, or why not? If you answered "yes," what kind of business would you like to have?
2   What are some advantages and disadvantages of being a business owner?
3   What kind of person do you have to be to start and run your own business?

B **Discuss your answers with a partner.**

Reading Skill
Making Inferences

Information in a reading passage is not always stated directly. Sometimes a reader has to infer (make guesses about) events, information, or a writer's opinion, using information in the reading.

A **Skim the first paragraph of the passage on the next page to answer the following question. You will have to infer information from the passage. Underline the sentences in the first paragraph that helped you find the answer.**

Which is considered the most common career path?
   a   go to university, then get a job afterwards
   b   start a business while in university
   c   start a business after university

B **Skim the rest of the passage, then read the sentences below. Circle the sentence that best describes the secret behind each person's success.**

Brian Laoruangroch
   a   Sell products from your own store or website to save money.
   b   Find the simplest way to sell your products, even if you have to pay extra for the service.

Whitney Williams
   a   Fall in love with someone who has the same interests as you.
   b   Spending time on your work now will help you be successful later.

Zac Workman
   a   Start small and let your company grow.
   b   Think big and don't listen to people who tell you "No."

C **Now read the entire passage carefully. Then answer the questions on page 100.**

Motivational Tip: Setting goals. Set a goal for your own personal reading rate on the next reading passage. When we set a goal, we have something to work toward. The goal must be realistic but challenging. When you work toward and achieve your reading rate goals, you will feel a great sense of satisfaction.

College Start-Ups

Most college students see their time at university as the first step in their career path; afterwards, they will go out into the working world

5 and get a job. But some students have great ideas that simply cannot wait until graduation day. With many free **resources** and technologies available to them, more and more

10 university students are finding ways to start small businesses while they are still in school. Let's take a look at a few **enterprising** undergraduates and their companies.

Green Mobile

15 As a student at the University of Missouri, Brian Laoruangroch used to sell refurbished[1] cell phones on eBay as a hobby. But when Brian realized how much money he could make by buying, fixing, and reselling phones, he decided to create his own website to resell the phones. His parents loaned him money, and he received money from his local government to found a company called Green Mobile, which now has local **retail** stores and about 20 employees. Brian said balancing work and studies was challenging, but he didn't forget to pay attention in

20 class. "I was learning important business **concepts** while I was using them in my own business," he said.

Whitney Williams Collection

Whitney Williams has always been creative, and she enjoys making things in her spare time. While in elementary school, she sold handmade **stationery** to people in her neighborhood, and later she expanded her offerings to include one-of-a-kind purses. When Whitney visited Italy as a student at Texas Christian University, she fell in love with the handmade jewelry she saw there. It inspired her to start her own jewelry

25 business. Instead of partying with friends or traveling, Whitney spent most of her weekends for the next two years selling her high-quality jewelry at small shows and private sales. As a result, the Whitney Williams Collection is now produced and sold around the world. Whitney hopes to eventually **expand** her brand to include shoes, clothing, and accessories.

Punch

As a competitive swimmer, Zac Workman became very familiar with energy drinks. However, Zac found problems

30 with most energy drinks. They either tasted bad, used chemicals that weren't healthy, or made the user feel tired again when its sugary energy was used up. This **spurred** Zac to do some research when he got to the University of Indiana. Using an old family recipe for fruit punch, Zac developed an energy drink with natural ingredients, and found a partner to produce it. His energy drink, called Punch, became popular on his **campus**. As his business grows, Zac says he's learning on the job. "People would think it would be difficult to balance class and a

35 business," he said, "but I'm learning more now than I ever have in the classroom."

[1] Something that is **refurbished** is made clean, fresh, or like new again.

Reading Comprehension
Check Your Understanding

A Choose the correct answers for the following questions.

1 According to the article, how many employees does Green Mobile have?
 a only one
 b about 20
 c over 30
2 Who did Whitney sell her first products to?
 a her neighbors
 b her classmates
 c her teachers
3 Which best describes Zac's energy drink Punch?
 a a drink made especially for swimmers
 b an all-natural drink that helps athletes
 c a fresh sports drink that Zac made every day

B Complete the diagram by writing the letter in the correct area.

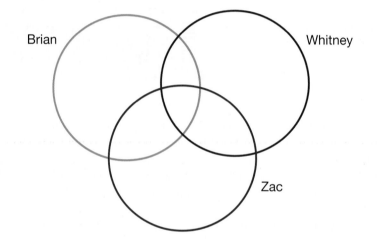

a turned a hobby into a business
b developed a product for athletes
c used family money to start the company
d says lessons learned in school have helped in managing a business
e started the company while still in university
f creates new and original products to sell
g worked weekends and did not see friends very often when starting the company

Critical Thinking

C Discuss the following questions with a partner.

1 Do you think a university student knows enough to start and manage a business? Why?
2 Should a business owner be more interested in making money or doing what they are passionate about? Why?

Vocabulary Comprehension
Definitions

A **Match each word with its definition. The words in blue are from the passage.**

1 ___ resource   **a** able to make money from new, interesting ideas
2 ___ enterprising   **b** products used for writing letters and notes
3 ___ retail   **c** money, skills, or time that is available when needed
4 ___ concept   **d** to get bigger
5 ___ stationery   **e** the land and buildings of a university or college
6 ___ expand   **f** concerning the sale of things to people in stores
7 ___ spur   **g** motivate, inspire
8 ___ campus   **h** an idea about how something is or should be done

B **Complete the following sentences using words from A. You might have to change the form of the word.**

1 I'd like to have a(n) _____ business selling personalized notebooks, but I don't have the _____ to start one!
2 The school decided to _____ the size of its _____ so that more students could attend.
3 Don't be afraid to fail. Sometimes that can _____ you on to great success.
4 Mr. Galison is very _____ ; his business _____ always seem to earn lots of money for the company.

Vocabulary Skill
Compound Nouns

A **Match a word from the box with a word below to make a compound noun.**

> computer   travel   book   taxi   police   fire   office   car   hair

1 _____ manager   2 _____ agent   3 _____ dealer
4 _____ programmer   5 _____ dresser   6 _____ driver
7 _____ fighter   8 _____ keeper   9 _____ officer

B **Which word(s) in A are one word? Which are two words? Discuss with a partner. You can use your dictionary to help you.**

C **Write the occupations from A next to the definitions below.**

	Occupation	Definition
1	_____	protects your city from criminals
2	_____	helps you with a vacation
3	_____	drives you from one place to another
4	_____	sells you a new automobile
5	_____	cuts and styles your hair
6	_____	creates websites or software
7	_____	puts out fires
8	_____	runs an office
9	_____	keeps a record of how much money a business has

> A compound noun joins two words to make one (for example, *hand* + *made* = *handmade*). Sometimes, two words are used to talk about one thing (for example, *retail store*). There are many compound nouns in English, and several are used to talk about jobs and careers.

CHAPTER 2 The Right Job for Your Personality

Before You Read
A Job That Fits You

A Think about each of these jobs. What kind of person is the best match for each job?

nurse

engineer

athlete

B Discuss your answers with a partner.

Reading Skill
Skimming for General Ideas

When we skim while reading, we read quickly to get a general idea of the meaning of the text. Later we can go back and read more slowly to understand all of the details.

A Look at the title of the article on the next page. Think of three words that describe your personality and write them here.

_____ _____ _____

B Skim the different personality groups in the article and quickly decide which group sounds the most similar to your personality. Circle the group in the box below.

Realistic	Investigative	Artistic
Social	Enterprising	Conventional

C Read the entire article carefully. Then answer the questions on page 104.

The Right Job for Your Personality

Choosing a career is an important life decision, yet many people settle on one based on the **opinions** of friends and family. It's very difficult to find something you really enjoy doing, but scientists have devised tests to help people come closer to finding their dream job.

One of the most widely-used tests is the Holland Code. Psychologist John Holland worked for more
5 than 50 years to develop his **theories** about personality and career choice. He created a set of six personality types to help people understand what careers might be best for them. Dr. Holland believed that people work best in environments that match their personalities, and the key to finding a satisfying career is to match your **fundamental** interests with an occupation.

Take a look at the six personality types below and see which jobs might be right for you. Most people
10 are a combination of two or three types.

Realistic

Realistic people like to work with things they can see or touch. They are **inclined to** solve problems by doing them, rather than thinking or talking about them. They generally like to work outside
15 and are good with tools, machines, plants, and animals.
Job matches: carpenter, chef, nurse, pilot

Investigative

People of this personality type value ideas and are strong at tasks that allow them to **investigate** facts and figure out complex problems. They are better at individual
20 work like research and study, rather than leading groups of people or working in teams.
Job matches: computer programmer, historian, psychologist, surgeon

Artistic

Artists are creative people. They don't work well with structure and rules, and **thrive** instead in environments that allow
25 communication and a free flow of ideas. They enjoy tasks that allow them to express themselves and mix with people.
Job matches: actor, art therapist, graphic designer, writer

Social

Social personalities love to
work with people. They get the most satisfaction out of teaching
30 and helping others, and are driven to serve the community as opposed to making money.
Job matches: coach, counselor, social worker, teacher

Enterprising

Many great leaders and business people have enterprising personalities. These are **persuasive** people who are good at
35 making decisions and leading teams. They tend to value money, power, and status, and will work toward achieving them.
Job matches: business owner, event manager, lawyer, salesperson

40 ### Conventional

Conventional people appreciate rules and **regulations**, and like having structure to their lives. They are logical thinkers and have a lot of self-control, making them the perfect people to work with data and details.
Job matches: accountant, analyst, editor, librarian

Nowadays, anyone can take a Holland Code personality test online to find what jobs might be right for
45 them. Why not try it today?

Reading Comprehension
Check Your Understanding

A Match the personality type with the description.

1 _____ Realistic   **a** likes to lead and influence other people
2 _____ Investigative   **b** likes to organize things and check details
3 _____ Artistic   **c** likes to create new things and express their ideas
4 _____ Social   **d** likes to work with their bodies and do practical things
5 _____ Enterprising   **e** likes to work with ideas and problems
6 _____ Conventional   **f** likes to work with and help other people

B Read the following sentences. Check (✓) true (*T*) or false (*F*).

	T	F
1 A person can fit into several personality types.		
2 Realistic and Conventional people like working with objects.		
3 Most people consider their personality type before choosing a job.		
4 Both Social and Investigative types like working with other people.		
5 You need to see an expert to take a Holland Code test.		

Critical Thinking

C Discuss the following question with a partner.

1 Can you suggest another job for each personality type that isn't already in the passage? Give reasons for your choices.
2 Do you think personality tests are accurate? Why, or why not?

Vocabulary Comprehension
Odd Word Out

A Circle the word or phrase that does not belong in each group. The words in blue are from the passage.

1 popular	decision	opinion	agreement
2 guess	hypothesis	politics	theory
3 fundamental	essential	central	mistaken
4 take care of	inclined to	support	encourage
5 investigate	find out about	study	ignore
6 succeed	prosper	thrive	reduce
7 romantic	forceful	strong	persuasive
8 order	error	regulation	law

B Answer the following questions, then discuss your answers with a partner. The words in blue are from the passage.

1 What are some jobs in which people investigate things? Would you enjoy doing these jobs?
2 What is the best way to persuade someone to do something?
3 Do you consider yourself an opinionated person? How so?
4 Do you think regulations are important in a job? Why, or why not?

A Look at some of the adjectives that describe people's personalities. Note the different adjective endings.

> introvert**ed** adventur**ous** responsi**ble** creat**ive**
> pati**ent** energe**tic** hard-work**ing**

B Complete the online job ads below with the appropriate adjective endings. Use your dictionary to help you.

JOBS AVAILABLE

Looking for a **(1)** self-motivat_____ and **(2)** effect_____ teacher to join the staff at our elementary school. You must have a teaching certificate and at least five years' experience to apply. Must also be **(3)** interest_____ in working with children ages 6–9.

(Read more >>)

Want to make $5,000 a month working in shorts and a T-shirt? Water World, the swimming pool specialist, has an immediate opening for an **(4)** adventur_____ and **(5)** assert_____ salesperson in the Boston area.

(Read more >>)

We have an immediate job opening for an **(6)** experienc_____, **(7)** flex_____ secretary in our very busy downtown office.

(Read more >>)

ScorePro, a software company that creates fun and educational math materials for children, is looking for a **(8)** dynam_____, **(9)** enthusiast_____ computer programmer to join our company.

(Read more >>)

C Choose one of the ads above. Using adjectives, think of two or three reasons to describe why you would be good for the job. Share your answers with a partner.

Motivational Tip: Reflect on your goals. Think back to the goal that you set for yourself at the beginning of this unit. Did you achieve your goal? Why, or why not? If you achieved your goal, find a way to celebrate! If you did not achieve your goal, determine what you need to do in the next unit to reach it and then celebrate.

Real Life Skill
Searching for a Job Online

Jobs listed on many websites are often organized by category; teaching jobs, for example, will often be listed within the category *Education*. Understanding job categories and recognizing key vocabulary in English can help you to begin a directed and successful online job search.

A Look at the career categories on the left. What kind of jobs might you find in each? Match the jobs with the categories.

1 _____ Administrative
2 _____ Education
3 _____ Finance
4 _____ Food, Travel, Hospitality
5 _____ Health Care
6 _____ Computer
7 _____ Legal
8 _____ Retail Sales and Marketing

a lawyer
b clothing salesperson
c nurse
d bank officer
e English teacher
f secretary
g web designer
h hotel manager

B How much do you want to work? Match a contract type with a definition.

a full-time   b part-time   c contract/temporary (temp)

1 _____ works about 5–20 hours per week
2 _____ works for a company for a specific period of time, e.g. 1 month
3 _____ a regular employee of a company; works 40+ hours per week

C Choose a job that is interesting to you, and the type of contract you would like. Go to one of the websites below and find a job that matches these requirements. Complete the information below.

www.careerbuilder.com   www.monster.com   www.workhound.co.uk

Website: _____

Job Description (title, location, pay, working hours):

_____

_____

_____

_____

What do you think?

Discuss the following questions with a partner.
1 Describe your ideal job.
2 Is it easy or difficult to find a job in your country? Why?
3 What advice have you heard for getting a job? Do you think these ideas are useful?

The Story of Chocolate

Getting Ready

Discuss the following questions with a partner.

1 What kinds of food and drink are made from chocolate?
2 How often do you eat chocolate? What kinds of chocolate do you like to eat?
3 Do you think eating chocolate is good or bad for you? Why?

CHAPTER 1 A Brief History of Chocolate

Before You Read
What do you know about chocolate?

A (Circle) the correct answer to complete each sentence.

1 Cacao plants only grow in (warm / cold) weather.
2 Chocolate is made from (leaves / seeds).
3 Chocolate can be deadly for (dogs / babies).
4 People first consumed chocolate by (drinking / eating) it.
5 *Theobroma cacao* is the scientific name for chocolate, and it means
(*food of the gods* / *glorious medicine food*).
6 White chocolate contains (a lot of / no) cocoa powder.
7 For every bar of chocolate eaten in China, there are (100 / 1,000) bars
eaten in the United Kingdom.
8 The most popular way to consume chocolate today is as (chocolate milk /
a chocolate bar).

B Discuss your answers with a partner. Then check your answers at the
bottom of page 109.

Reading Skill
Recognizing Sequence of Events

Not all articles present events in order; sometimes a writer will introduce a main idea or event before explaining how or why it happened. To show time relationships, writers use words like *originally*, *later*, and *today*.

A Read the sentences below, then scan the passage on the next page for
the information. (Circle) the event that happened first.

1 a Chocolate became popular in Spain.
  b Chocolate became popular in France.
2 a Chocolate was used in ceremonies.
  b Chocolate was fashionable.
3 a Chocolate tasted sweet.
  b Chocolate tasted bitter.
4 a Chocolate was eaten.
  b Chocolate was drunk.

B Which words or phrases in the passage helped you understand the
order of the events in A? Write them below.

1 _____
2 _____
3 _____
4 _____

C Now read the entire passage carefully. Then answer the questions on
page 110.

A Brief History of Chocolate

One of the most beloved foods in the world, chocolate is not just a modern treat. In fact, chocolate—or rather, cacao seeds—has been part of our **culinary** history for thousands of years.

5   More than 2,000 years ago in Central America, the Mayan people began **consuming** a drink made from cacao seeds. There was no sugar in America in those days, and so they flavored the drink with chili peppers and other spices. It was called *xocolatl*, meaning *bitter water*. The Mayans used *xocolatl* for important rituals, such as religious ceremonies or weddings, and believed that

10 consuming it would **enhance** their health and **cure** illnesses. Caco seeds became highly valued throughout Central America, and were even used as currency[1] by the Aztecs.

Hernando Cortez

On his fourth voyage to America in 1502, the explorer Christopher Columbus landed in what is now called Nicaragua. He was the first European to discover cacao seeds being used as money, but he did not consider it very significant. It was only later, in the 16th century, that another   15 explorer, Hernando Cortez, saw cacao's value, and brought the drink and the **equipment** used to make it back to Spain. The Spanish didn't quite take to the bitter taste, and added other ingredients such as sugar and vanilla, so that chocolate more closely **resembled** the sweet treat we know today.   20

As popular as chocolate was in Spain, it didn't spread to the rest of Europe until nearly a hundred years later, when a Spanish princess married the French king and made chocolate fashionable. By the 17th century, the chocolate drink had gained widespread popularity in France,

25 and an ambitious Frenchman opened the first chocolate house in London. Soon, chocolate drinks were sold everywhere in London, and English bakers began using it in cakes—the first mention of chocolate being eaten and not drunk.

But the biggest development in modern chocolate consumption happened by accident in 1828. C. J. Van Houten, a Dutch chemist, discovered a method for making powdered chocolate when he

30 tried to **extract** oils from cacao to make the drink smoother. This product became known as "cocoa powder." Not long after, in 1847, a British man named Joseph Fry developed "eating chocolate," which were chocolate bars made of cocoa powder, cocoa butter, and sugar. This led to the first milk chocolate bars, sold by Nestlé, a Swiss company. These were created by adding condensed milk[2] to Fry's chocolate bar recipe. Fry's company, Fry & Sons, was later bought by Cadbury. Today, Nestlé and

35 Cadbury remain the world's leading chocolate producers.

Chocolate hasn't lost its popularity, and has yet to stop **evolving**. Stop in your local specialty chocolate shop and you might find chocolates filled with fruit jellies and even flower petals. Food scientists have made chocolate sauces that can harden in seconds, and chocolate bars that don't melt in hot weather. For people who cannot live without chocolate, scientists have added the smell

40 and taste to products like soap, perfume, toothpaste, and lipstick. As world-famous chocolatier Jacques Torres once said, "Chocolate is a magical product."

---

[1] The money used in a particular country is referred to as its **currency**.
[2] **Condensed milk** is cow's milk with water removed, and usually has added sugar.

Reading Comprehension
Check Your Understanding

A Choose the correct answers for the following questions.

1   Which is another possible title for the passage?
    a   How Chocolate Moved Around the World
    b   Cooking with Chocolate in Different Cultures
    c   Modern Ways of Making and Eating Chocolate
2   Which is NOT mentioned as a use for chocolate?
    a   money
    b   medicine
    c   decoration
3   What is the purpose of talking about C.J. Van Houten?
    a   to teach readers how to make cocoa powder
    b   to explain why Europeans first liked chocolate
    c   to show how modern chocolate developed

B Read the following sentences. Check (✓) true (T) or false (F).

		T	F
1	Christopher Columbus knew that cacao seeds were used as currency.		
2	For many years, chocolate was only popular in France.		
3	C.J. Van Houten did not intend to make cocoa powder.		
4	Modern chocolate bars were invented by one person.		
5	Nestle and Cadbury are still some of the most successful chocolate producers.		

Critical Thinking

C Discuss the following questions with a partner.

1   How do you think chocolate tasted when the Mayans and Aztecs prepared it? Would you like to drink this kind of chocolate? Why, or why not?
2   Why do you think chocolate remains such a popular food?

Motivational Tip: A valuable life-skill. Thinking critically about what you've just read is an important way to learn beyond the textbook. How can this critical thinking help in your personal life?

Vocabulary Comprehension
Words in Context

A Choose the best answer. The words in blue are from the passage.

1   Which would be taught in a culinary class?
    a   how to make flowers grow   b how to cut a potato
2   Which of the following would you consume?
    a   a sandwich   b   a shirt

3 When you enhance something, you make it _____ .
    a better   **b** worse

4 What can you cure?
    a a mistake   **b** a headache

5 What can you extract from a watermelon?
    a juice   **b** skin

6 Which are examples of soccer equipment?
    a ball, shoes   **b** players, coach

7 When something evolves, it _____ .
    a changes   **b** stays the same

8 If you resemble your father, you _____ him.
    a respect   **b** look like

B **Answer the following questions, then discuss your answers with a partner. The words in blue are from A.**

1 Do you have any culinary skills? Who did you learn them from?
2 Name an invention that has evolved over time.
3 Name something that needs a cure.
4 Have you ever been told you resemble someone famous? Who?

A **Look at the underlined word in each sentence. Write down the part of speech (*noun, verb, adjective, adverb, etc.*) for each word.**

1 There was no sugar in America in those days, and so they <u>flavored</u> the drink with chili peppers and other spices.
    Part of speech: _____
    Meaning: _____

2 The Mayans used xocolatl for important <u>rituals</u>, such as religious ceremonies or weddings.
    Part of speech: _____
    Meaning: _____

3 The Spanish didn't quite <u>take to</u> the bitter taste, and added other ingredients such as sugar and vanilla
    Part of speech: _____
    Meaning: _____

4 Stop in your local <u>specialty</u> chocolate shop and you might find chocolates filled with fruit jellies and even flower petals.
    Part of speech: _____
    Meaning: _____

Vocabulary Skill
Identifying Part of Speech

> Knowing which part of speech a word is can help you to understand its meaning. Other words in a sentence can also help you to understand the meaning of new vocabulary.

B **Write the meaning of the underlined words, and ⟨circle⟩ the words in the sentence that helped you to understand the meaning.**

C **Discuss your answers with a partner.**

Before You Read

Is Chocolate Bad for You?

A Think about answers to the following questions.

1 What are some bad things that you have heard about eating chocolate?
2 Can you think of books or movies that feature chocolate? How is chocolate described in the media?
3 Do you think chocolate has a good or bad reputation? Why?

B Discuss your answers with a partner.

Reading Skill

Understanding the Main Ideas

> Understanding the main ideas of each paragraph in a reading can help you to follow the argument the author is making, and to understand the main idea of the whole passage.

A Skim the paragraphs numbered 1–5 in the article on the next page. Then read the sentences below and check (✓) if they are true (*T*), somewhat true (*S*), or false (*F*).

		T	S	F
1	Eating chocolate makes you happier.			
2	Chocolate makes you fat.			
3	Chocolate is good for your heart.			
4	Chocolate gives you pimples.			
5	Chocolate causes tooth decay.			

B Now write one detail from the passage that supports your answer for each of the paragraphs.

Paragraph 1: _____

Paragraph 2: _____

Paragraph 3: _____

Paragraph 4: _____

Paragraph 5: _____

C Read the entire passage again carefully. Then answer the questions on page 114.

> **Motivational Tip: Strengthen your personal relationships.** Your friends can help you achieve your reading goals. Sharing your goals can also strengthen your personal relationships. As you begin this unit, share with a friend what you hope to learn in this unit about chocolate that will help you become a better user of English.

The Truth about Chocolate

If you ever **crave** chocolate, you're not alone—millions of people around the world admit to being "chocolate addicts." But have you wondered if this addiction is damaging to your health? Let's separate the myths from the facts concerning this popular food.

① Eating chocolate makes you happier.

5 It's not your imagination. Chocolate contains over 300 known chemicals, which **stimulate** areas of the brain that enable us to feel pleasure. Chocolate contains small amounts of theobromine, which help to enhance your mood, and caffeine, which gives you more energy and is also found in coffee and tea.

② Chocolate makes you fat.

Chocolate is commonly regarded as a fattening food that contains no **nutritional** value. In fact, cocoa beans
10 are full of antioxidants that are beneficial to health. However, they **undergo** a lot of processing to remove their **distinctive** bitterness, which also removes a large portion of the antioxidants. Most store-bought chocolates have high sugar and fat content, and only small amounts of cocoa. Eating these and other high-calorie chocolate desserts, like cakes and cookies, can indeed cause you to gain weight.

③ Chocolate is good for your heart.

15 There have been studies in recent years linking chocolate to a healthy heart. Cocoa contains chemicals called flavanols which fight heart disease by lowering blood pressure and cholesterol levels. But you'll have to consume dark chocolate with a high proportion of cocoa if you want to see the benefits,
20 or just eat more fruits and vegetables, which contain flavanols as well and in higher amounts. "If you want to reduce your heart disease risk, there are much better places to start than at the bottom of a box of chocolates," says Victoria Taylor from the British Heart Foundation.

④ Chocolate gives you pimples.

25 Despite what you might have heard from your mother or grandmother, there is absolutely no evidence that chocolate gives you pimples or acne. It's not chocolate that causes problems, but the highly-processed **nature** of the products containing chocolate, and their high levels of sugar and fat. While it's great that chocolate isn't to blame, bad skin could still indicate a bad diet.

⑤ Chocolate causes tooth decay.

30 This is another myth that just won't go away. It's not chocolate itself that causes tooth **decay**, but the sugar in chocolate products—and bad teeth-brushing habits! In fact, it is believed that cocoa butter forms a coating over our teeth, and this might actually protect rather than hurt them.

As with most things, chocolate only becomes a danger when you overdo it. It's important to remember that
35 most of the health benefits of chocolate come from cocoa, which is why dark chocolate is the healthiest option. So choose your chocolate wisely, eat it in **moderation**, and you'll get the best of both worlds— happiness AND health.

Reading Comprehension
Check Your Understanding

A **Choose the correct answer for the following questions.**

1 Most commercial chocolates contain lots of _____.
   a antioxidants
   b cocoa
   c sugar

2 What does Victoria Taylor mean in her quote in lines 21–23?
   a She thinks chocolates are actually bad for your heart.
   b There are better things out there to help prevent heart disease.
   c Most boxes of chocolate only contain white or milk chocolates.

3 Why does the writer mention *mother and grandmother* in line 26?
   a to show that chocolates causing pimples is an old belief
   b to show that modern chocolates don't cause pimples
   c to show that women tend to get pimples from eating chocolate

B **Read the following sentences. Check (✓) if they are shown as positive (+) or negative (–) in the article.**

		+	–
1	Chemicals in chocolate can change our emotions.		
2	Most people eat chocolate in candy bars and cakes.		
3	Cocoa beans are processed to remove their bitter taste.		
4	Chocolate contains flavanols.		
5	When eaten, cocoa butter can coat the teeth.		

Critical Thinking

C **Discuss the following questions with a partner.**

1 In your opinion, how often is it healthy to eat chocolate?
2 Why do you think modern chocolates have so much sugar and fat?

Vocabulary Comprehension
Definitions

A **Match each word with its definition. The words in blue are from the passage.**

1	_____ decay	**a**	very different or special
2	_____ crave	**b**	to rot or slowly be destroyed
3	_____ distinctive	**c**	the basic character or quality of something
4	_____ stimulate	**d**	to excite or make something more active
5	_____ nutritional	**e**	related to the vitamins, minerals, etc., in food
6	_____ nature	**f**	in healthy or reasonable amounts
7	_____ moderation	**g**	to experience something
8	_____ undergo	**h**	to want something very much

B **Complete the following sentences with the correct form of the words from A.**

1 Women's diets tend to _____ a change when they get pregnant, and they may start _____ foods they've never liked before.

2 This dish has a very _____ taste—it's sweet and sour at the same time.

3 People are not allowed to keep tigers as pets because it's in their _____ to be aggressive, and they might harm their owners.

4 Keep healthy by eating fresh fruit, vegetables and other _____ foods, and consuming oily or salty foods in _____ .

A Read the article below and find synonyms for the vocabulary definitions in the following chart.

Health News

It's accepted that exercising regularly is good for health. But is too much of it a good thing? A recent report in a leading medical journal may have proof that exercising too much can in fact be dangerous. When we work out, we get a lift or "high" from chemicals released into the brain. It is this "high" that people become addicted to, and it can have negative effects on body and mind.

Over-exercisers may find their muscles are constantly sore; some may even get stress fractures, or small cracks in their bones, from doing intense workouts. A person obsessed with exercising day after day can end up feeling exhausted all the time. They may also feel restless or unable to sleep at night. If you find yourself weaker instead of stronger after working out, it may be evidence of over-exercising. But those who are hooked on exercise should not quit altogether. Doctors advise to slowly cut back on the number of days a week that you exercise, and to limit yourself to only an hour a day.

Vocabulary Skill
Synonyms

A synonym is a word that has the same or similar meaning as another word. One way of increasing your vocabulary is by learning synonyms.

Definitions	Synonyms
bad for you	
dependent on something	
information to show that something is true	
happening all the time	
tired	
to reduce or lessen	

B Write one more synonym for each definition. Then discuss your answers with a partner.

Real Life Skill

Dictionary Usage:
Choosing the Right
Dictionary Definition

When you look up
words in a dictionary
you will sometimes
see more than one
definition. You can use
the example sentence
in the dictionary, or the
sentence in the book you
are reading, to help you
decide which definition is
the right one to use.

A Look at the dictionary entries below. Then read the following sentences and decide which definition is correct. Write *1* or *2* next to each sentence.

consume *v.* **1** to eat and drink; **2** to destroy

contribute *v.* **1** to give or donate something (time, money, etc.); **2** to help make something successful

cultivate *v.* **1** to prepare land for growing crops, trees, and flowers; plowing, planting seeds, and fertilizing soil; **2** to study and develop a good understanding of something (books, art, music)

1 _____ Fire consumed the entire restaurant in less than an hour. Fortunately, all the diners and staff escaped unhurt.

2 _____ Each person in the office contributed $10 to help pay the hospital bill for their sick colleague.

3 _____ Steven cultivated his knowledge of Asian culture while taking many business trips to Korea and Japan.

B Now write three more sentences using the other definitions of the words above.

1 _____

_____

2 _____

_____

3 _____

_____

What do you think?

1 Chocolate is described as a food that has evolved over time. Can you think of other foods that have evolved?

2 Can you think of other foods that have myths surrounding them?

3 Are there any foods that you "can't live without"?

You can ask yourself three questions to improve your reading fluency and comprehension. The letters K, W, and L can be used to remind you of these questions.
KWL stands for **K**now, **W**ant, **L**earn.

Know

The first step in KWL is similar to the Preview step in PRO (page 41) and the A in the Active approach (inside front cover). This step will help you prepare yourself before reading.

A Look at the title of the passage on the next page, *Will Shortz: Puzzle Maker*. Then read only the first paragraph of the passage. From the title and first paragraph, decide what is the topic of the passage.

B Ask yourself, "What do I already know about this topic?" Write down three or four facts that you already know about the topic in the Know column of the table below.

Know	Want	Learn

Want

In the second stage of KWL, ask yourself, "What do I **want** to learn as I read?" By doing this you are reading with a purpose. This step is similar to the Question stage in PQR+E.

A Ask yourself what you want to learn as you read *Will Shortz: Puzzle Maker*. Write down some things you hope to learn in the Want column above.

B Before going on to the L in KWL, read the passage on the next page carefully.

Will Shortz: Puzzle Maker

When you ask a child what they would like to be when they grow up, common responses might include firefighter, pilot, doctor, or athlete. But those jobs don't capture the attention of all kids. Take Will

5   Shortz, for example. In eighth grade, at the age of 14, Will had to write an essay about what he wanted to do with his life. He wrote about his desire to become a puzzle maker—someone who creates games and puzzles, such as sudoku or crossword puzzles. That

10 same year, he sold his first puzzle to the magazine *Venture*. By the age of 16, Will was regularly contributing puzzles to magazines.

In college, Will found that there was no traditional way to study puzzles or become a puzzle maker. There were no classes offered on puzzles. Fortunately, after becoming bored with his economics studies, Will learned that his university offered a special program that allowed students to suggest and

15 create unique fields of study. After creating and completing two courses on word and math puzzles, Will switched his major to enigmatology—the study of puzzles.

Will and his professors then created new classes that explored all aspects of puzzle-making. He studied the history, construction, and psychology of puzzles, mostly on his own. Because there were no professors of enigmatology, Will realized that he probably was the only student at his

20 university to know more about his field than any of his professors!

He did well in school, but upon graduating, Will did not know how to get a job creating puzzles. For summer work, he joined the magazine *Penny Press*, where he realized that he could find work as a puzzle editor. Will then found a job creating and editing puzzles for *Games* magazine. This seemed like a dream job because he could create new kinds of puzzles and be surrounded by great puzzle

25 makers.

After 15 years at *Games*, Will accepted a position as the editor of *The New York Times*' crossword puzzle. When he first joined, the newspaper's crossword puzzle was seen as very difficult, and few readers could complete it. Will made fundamental changes, such as including everyday language in the clues and answers so that many more people could enjoy it. Today, he

30 is credited with making the crossword appealing to a wider audience. Some of Will's most famous puzzles have related to the news for that day, such as the name of the winning president on Election Day, and a love-themed puzzle on Valentine's Day.

Learn

Now that you have finished reading, ask yourself, "What did I **learn** while reading?" Did you learn what you wanted to?

A **Write down three or four things you learned about Will Shortz in the *Learn* column of the chart on page 117.**

B **Now test how much you learned from the passage by answering the following questions.**

1 The writer mentions other children in the introduction to show _____.
   a how every child has a different ambition
   b how Will Shortz was different from other children
   c that they were not interested in puzzles
   d that none of them were as successful as Will Shortz

2 When did Will first become interested in puzzles?
   a before he was 14 years old
   b when he was 14 years old
   c when he was 16 years old
   d when he entered university

3 What kind of classes did Will Shortz take in college?
   a classes by professors who study puzzle-writing
   b classes that he and his professors developed
   c classes taught by professional puzzle makers
   d classes that art students take

4 Which sentence describes Will Shortz's college experience?
   a He enjoyed his time in college very much.
   b He was bored in college and did not finish.
   c He felt he did not learn very much.
   d He thought it was too challenging.

5 Why is *Penny Press* mentioned in the fourth paragraph?
   a It is the first company at which Will Shortz worked.
   b It is where he was allowed to develop new puzzles.
   c The owner of the company did not hire Will Shortz.
   d It is where Will Shortz worked during college.

6 Why did Will Shortz consider his job at *Games* magazine a "dream job"?
   a He earned a lot of money writing crossword puzzles.
   b *Games* was the only puzzle magazine in the U.S.
   c He could study the history of puzzle-making at the magazine.
   d He designed new puzzles and worked with other puzzle makers.

7 At *The New York Times*, Will Shortz _____.
   a changed the kind of puzzle the newspaper published
   b made the crossword puzzle more interesting for most people
   c made the crossword puzzle more difficult to solve
   d wrote newspaper articles about puzzles and games

SELF CHECK

Answer the following questions.

1 Have you ever used the KWL method before?

☐ Yes   ☐ No   ☐ *I'm not sure.*

2 Will you practice KWL in your reading outside of English class?

☐ Yes   ☐ No   ☐ *I'm not sure.*

3 Do you think KWL is helpful? Why, or why not?

_____

_____

4 Which of the six reading passages in units 7–9 did you enjoy most? Why?

_____

_____

5 Which of the six reading passages in units 7–9 was easiest? Which was the most difficult? Why?

_____

_____

6 What have you read in English outside of class recently?

_____

_____

7 What time of day do you most feel like reading? Do you use that part of the day to do your most important reading and studying?

_____

_____

8 Are you keeping a vocabulary journal?

_____

_____

Review Reading 5: The People Behind the Music

Fluency Practice

Time yourself as you read through the passage. Try to read as fluently as you can. Record your time in the Reading Rate Chart on page 176. Then answer the questions on the next page.

The People Behind the Music

Think for a moment about the last music album you bought. Most likely, you'll think of the singer or band that made you want to buy the album. You might even know the name of the guitar player or the drummer. Those talented performers, however, are only some of the people involved in making the music you enjoy. The majority of people in the music industry work behind the scenes,
5   but the roles they play in the musical process are very important.

Songwriters

Songs begin with the songwriter, of course. Some songwriters work alone, but many work in teams that combine the talents of a lyricist, who writes the words to songs, and an instrumentalist, often a piano player or guitarist, who writes the music. Many of today's pop stars work with songwriters. For example, some
10   of Lady Gaga's biggest hits were written by Nadir Khayat, also known as "RedOne." Some songwriting teams have become very famous, such as Mike Stock, Matt Aitken, and Pete Waterman, who were responsible for many big '80s pop hits.

Arrangers

After a song has been written, music arrangers make it more appealing by deciding which instruments will be used,
15   what tempo, or speed, the song will have, and whether the song should have a lower or higher pitch. A good arrangement can bring a song to life and make it a classic.

Studio Musicians

Not every singer or instrumentalist can be a star, and many work in the background as studio musicians. These artists are not a part of any one musical group. Instead, they are hired for recording sessions that eventually become the
20   albums you buy, as well as soundtracks for television shows, movies, and radio ads.

Recording Engineers

Recording engineers also play a major role in creating the final sound that you hear. First, these engineers set up the recording studio, the room where the performers play, placing musicians and microphones in exactly the right places to get the best
25   sound. Next, they use electronic equipment, such as multi-track recorders, to capture the music. Finally, long after the musicians have gone home, recording engineers use a mixing board to balance the melodies and rhythms of each musician,
30   and sometimes to incorporate special sound effects or additional tracks.

Many people make a living with music. You may not recognize all of their names, but all of them work together to create the songs you love to listen to.

405 words   **Time taken** _____

Reading Comprehension

1 The article is mainly about _____ .
   a pop stars who write the biggest hits
   b songwriting teams who combine their talents
   c people who play a background role in creating music
   d instrumentalists who work as hired musicians

2 According to the passage, an instrumentalist is responsible for _____ .
   a writing the music of a song
   b writing the lyrics of a song
   c choosing piano and guitar players
   d recording the music

3 Why does the author mention Lady Gaga?
   a to give an example of a star who works with a songwriter
   b to explain why she does not write her own songs
   c to compare her with other talented songwriters
   d to persuade readers to buy her music

4 Which of the following do music arrangers probably NOT do?
   a decide which pitch to use
   b decide how fast or slow a song will be
   c decide which instruments to use
   d decide the price of the CD

5 Which piece of equipment is used at the end of the recording process?
   a a guitar or piano
   b a microphone
   c a mixing board
   d a multi-track recorder

6 Which sentence is NOT true about studio musicians?
   a They work in the recording studio.
   b They are not as famous as the artists they play for.
   c They usually support or play for the same artist.
   d They earn money for each session that they do.

7 Which statement would the author probably agree with?
   a Studio musicians would be more successful as members of one musical group.
   b It is important to buy albums made by performing artists who are not yet famous.
   c People are often unaware of the amount of work that goes into creating music.
   d Having a famous person sing a song will usually make it successful.

Review Reading 6: Savory Chocolate

Fluency Practice

Time yourself as you read through the passage. Try to read as fluently as you can. Record your time in the Reading Rate Chart on page 176. Then answer the questions on the next page.

Candy, cake, brownies, ice cream, pie, fudge—these are some common uses for chocolate. But did you know that chocolate also has a savory[1] side? Michael Laiskonis, a pastry chef, says that while chocolate is certainly thought of most often as a sweet snack or dessert, it is being used more frequently in savory dishes.

Cocoa, and later chocolate, was first enjoyed by the Mayans and Aztecs of Central America, and then by the Europeans, particularly in countries like Spain, Portugal, and Italy. It makes sense, then, that many savory chocolate dishes can be found in these cuisines, most commonly in their sauces. This is because chocolate adds a dark, shiny color and a rich flavor to the sauce.

a mole dish

Mexican *moles* are a good example of sauces that heavily feature chocolate. Moles are rich and spicy sauces that originated in southern Mexico around the 16th and 17th centuries. They get their complex flavor and dark brown color from chili peppers and chocolate, much like the original cocoa drinks from Mayan times. Moles are commonly served with meat and rice. Over in Europe, an Italian wine or vinegar sauce called *agrodolce* also uses chocolate, and is most often served with lamb and pasta. Some recipes for *coq au vin,* a classic French chicken dish, call for chocolate as well.

Chocolate is being used in less traditional dishes, too. Chefs and home cooks alike are rubbing steaks with cocoa powder and adding pieces of chocolate to meat stews. Many recipes follow the Mexican idea of adding cocoa or dark chocolate, which has a bitter flavor, to spicy dishes, but it has recently become very popular in America to cover salty bacon or potato chips in chocolate.

This combination sounds odd but can actually be explained through science. Studies called "flavor-study research" have shown that certain foods with similar chemical structures taste good when eaten together. For example, chef Heston Blumenthal combined white chocolate and caviar[2] because he thought the two offered a tasty balance of sweet and salty. Scientists later found that these two flavors go well together because they have some proteins in common. This is also the reason why scientists think cocoa tastes good with cauliflower and garlic.

This might all sound a little strange if you've only ever known chocolate to be a sweet treat. But it's also good news for chocolate lovers—as Laiskonis says, "No matter what your mother may have told you, it's perfectly acceptable to eat chocolate for dinner!"

[1] **Savory** food is food that does not taste sweet.
[2] If you eat raw eggs from the sturgeon fish, you are eating **caviar**.

414 words   **Time taken** _____

Reading Comprehension

1 The writer assumes that the reader _____ .
   a knows how to bake chocolate cake
   b knows chocolate is used in desserts
   c likes to eat chocolate in savory dishes
   d has traveled to Central America

2 Which question is NOT answered in the passage?
   a How is mole made?
   b What ingredients are in mole?
   c What color is mole?
   d When was mole first made?

3 What effect does chocolate have on dishes?
   a It makes the sauce darker.
   b It makes the dish sweeter.
   c It makes the meat softer.
   d It makes the dish spicier.

4 How does the article describe the flavor of cocoa powder?
   a bitter
   b sweet
   c salty
   d spicy

5 Which food is NOT mentioned as going well with chocolate?
   a cauliflower
   b garlic
   c caviar
   d apple

6 According to scientists, what determines if a food will taste good with chocolate?
   a the food's chemical structure
   b the food's level of sweetness
   c the food's color
   d the food's place of origin

7 When the writer says it is *good news for chocolate lovers* in lines 29–30, what is he referring to?
   a They now have more knowledge about chocolate.
   b They can eat as much chocolate as they like.
   c They now have an excuse to eat chocolate during meals.
   d They now know what goes well with chocolate.

The Secrets of Advertising

Sales people from Red Bull, an energy drink company, drive specially designed cars.

Advertising billboards are very common in the United States.

Big websites like YouTube make lots of money by featuring advertisements.

Getting Ready

Discuss the following questions with a partner.

1 Have you seen any advertising yesterday or today? Where? Check (✓) all that apply.

☐ on television   ☐ in newspapers   ☐ on public transportation
☐ on flyers   ☐ in store displays   ☐ on clothes
☐ in text messages   ☐ in emails   ☐ on websites

2 Which of these advertisements did you pay attention to? Why?

Before You Read
Interesting Ads

A **Look at these pictures and answer the following questions.**

1 Which shows a more traditional form of advertising, and which shows a more modern form? How are they different?

2 Which do you think is more effective in selling a product? Why?

B **Discuss your answers with a partner.**

Reading Skill
Scanning for Proper Nouns

One way to quickly recognize what a reading passage is about is by first scanning for proper nouns. Proper nouns are specific names of people, places, and things. They are easy to find because they start with capital letters.

A **Scan the passage on the next page for proper nouns. Write the proper nouns you find in each paragraph below. Then (circle) the correct option.**

Paragraph 2 _____
This paragraph is probably about (clothing / exercise).

Paragraph 3 _____
This paragraph is probably about (drinks people buy / entertainment).

Paragraph 5 _____
This paragraph is probably about (the Internet / animals).

B **Now skim the passage to see if your answers were correct.**

C **Read the entire passage carefully. Then answer the questions on page 128.**

Motivational Tip: Set a class goal. Together with your classmates, set a class goal for reading rate and reading comprehension for the two chapters in this unit. How many words-per-minute do you think your class can achieve? What level of comprehension can you achieve? Check to see if you have met your class goals at the end of this unit.

Ads Are Everywhere!

1 Would you believe that the average person sees nearly 3,000 ads every day? That seems unbelievable, but advertising has become so common that ads are **virtually** everywhere we look. Furthermore, most advertisements today don't seem like advertising. Newspapers and television are no longer the only
5 way for companies to reach their target audience. Today, advertisers are far more **subtle** in their selling.

2 Take a look: your clothes may have a brand name or logo on them. Many designer brands like Gucci and Louis Vuitton display their logo **prominently** on their clothes and bags. Branding is also very important
10 for big sports companies and professional sports teams. For example, Nike has spent hundreds of millions of dollars creating and promoting their instantly recognizable "swoosh" logo.

Tiger Woods wearing Nike clothes

3 Your favorite forms of entertainment are also filled with ads. Companies actively seek to sponsor concerts and TV shows: for example, the Coca-Cola Company has sponsored *American Idol*, one of the most popular shows
15 on American television, since its first season. Similarly, many sports tournaments would be impossible to hold if not for money given by sponsors, who want their ads clearly **visible** in stadiums. In movies, you'll see characters driving a particular brand of car, or eating a popular snack, because companies pay for their products to be there. In the James Bond film *Casino Royale*, car manufacturer Ford paid about $22 million for James Bond to drive one of its cars—for only three minutes!

4 20 The problem for advertisers is that people have learned to **ignore** traditional advertising, such as TV ads and billboards. Advertisers must find new ways to get the public to notice them—and continue noticing them. The key word now is "engagement": companies are trying to create deeper, more **interactive** experiences, which could be anything from contests to parties to charity runs, and link the experience with the brand.

5 Companies have starting using the Internet to reach a wider audience. For example, brand websites can be
25 **accessed** by anyone, anywhere. Advertisers are using social networking sites like Facebook to post videos and entertaining stories that feature the company's products. Their goal is for people to share these posts with their friends, and eventually reach millions of people. The energy drink company Red Bull has been very successful in creating online **content** that viewers respond to. By sponsoring and making short films focused on extreme sports like skateboarding and surfing, Red Bull has attracted more than hundreds of
30 millions of views on its YouTube channel.

6 Advertisers are finding new and different ways to grab our attention. As a results, ads are getting more creative. Instead of telling us what is so special about a product, advertisers are making products part of our lives.

Reading Comprehension
Check Your Understanding

A **Choose the correct answers for the following questions.**

1 The passage mentions clothing in paragraph 2 because _____.
   a consumers pay extra for clothing with logos
   b clothing can be a way to advertise a product
   c advertising on T-shirts does not work

2 Which best describes what the writer means by "engagement"?
   a A company puts an advertisment in the newspaper.
   b A company pays a famous actor to appear in a television commercial.
   c A company organizes and funds local sporting events.

3 According to the passage, what is the main problem advertisers face today?
   a Advertising costs too much money.
   b People do not notice advertisements anymore.
   c People do not read newspapers or watch TV anymore.

B **Circle the correct answers to complete the following sentences.**

1 Advertisers have (fewer / more) ways to reach consumers now.
2 In modern advertising, we (know / don't know) when we're being sold to.
3 Branding involves companies creating (memorable logos / better products).
4 (Ford / The movie studio) paid to have a specific car used in a James Bond movie.
5 Companies use social network sites like Facebook so that people can (share information about the brand / buy their product directly).
6 Red Bull sponsors short films about (energy drinks / skateboarding).

Critical Thinking

C **Discuss the following questions with a partner.**

1 Are there any places you think advertising should NOT appear? Why?
2 Do you prefer advertisements that educate and inform you, or do you prefer ones that entertain you? Why?

Vocabulary Comprehension
Words in Context

A **Choose the best answer. The words in blue are from the passage.**

1 The project is virtually finished, so there's _____ to do.
   a not much   b still a lot

2 When something is painted a subtle color, you _____ notice it.
   a immediately   b hardly

3 A prominent company is usually _____.
   a successful   b unsuccessful

4 One reason a store's sign might not be visible is that _____.
   a it has misspelled words   b it is too small

5 A man sits next to you. One way to ignore him is to _____.
   a start talking to him   b pretend he is not there

6 Which is a more interactive activity?
   a reading a book   **b** discussing a book with friends
7 If you get access to a building, you _____.
   a are allowed to enter it   **b** must leave it quickly
8 If you like a website's content, you like its _____.
   a words and pictures   **b** design

B **Answer the following questions, then discuss your answers with a partner. The words in blue are from the passage.**

1 Can you name a company with a famous logo? Describe the logo.
2 What kind of subtle clues could you give friends so they buy you the birthday gift you want?
3 How can students have more interaction within the classroom?

A **Write in-, im-, or un- next to the words in the box to make them negative.**

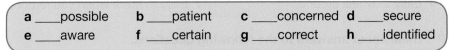

a ____possible   b ____patient   c ____concerned d ____secure
e ____aware   f ____certain   g ____correct   h ____identified

Vocabulary Skill
Prefixes *in-*, *im-*, and *un-*

B **Write the letters of words from A next to the correct definition.**

1 _____: not seeing or knowing something
2 _____: not confident about yourself
3 _____: not sure about something
4 _____: annoyed because you have to wait
5 _____: not worried or not interested
6 _____: wrong or untrue
7 _____: not recognized
8 _____: cannot happen or cannot be done

> You read the word *unbelievable* in line 2 of the reading passage. The prefixes *in-*, *im-*, and *un-* mean *not*, so adding them to a word makes it negative. These can come at the beginning of a verb, adjective, or adverb. Recognizing and remembering what these prefixes mean can help you to understand more words.

C **Use the prefixes *in-* and *un-* to complete the article below. Leave the space blank if the word doesn't need a prefix.**

Dressing Down in the Office

It's "Casual Friday" in the office, and you're wearing a pair of jeans and a sweater. This **(1)** _____formal style of dress in the workplace would not be considered **(2)** _____appropriate in today's business world. In fact, psychologists say that "dressing down" (as opposed to "dressing up") helps people be creative and **(3)** _____relaxed.

   (4) _____fortunately, many companies are doing away with "Casual Fridays." This is because most employees are **(5)** _____aware of what exactly "business casual" is, and come to work looking **(6)** _____tidy, dressed more for the beach than for the office. As a rule, avoid wearing slippers and shorts, and try to wear nice pants and shirts with collars. If you're **(7)** _____sure about your employer's rules, just ask!

CHAPTER 2 Brand Engagement Gone Wrong

Before You Read
Interesting Ads

Rett's Alligator Luggage

⇨ Unbreakable case
⇨ Comes in many attractive colors
⇨ Easy to wheel around

Clean-Up Kwik Set

⇨ Everything you need to clean the house
⇨ Pretty and color-coordinated
⇨ Easy to store when you're done

A **Think about answers to the following questions.**

    1   What kind of customers would buy the products above?

    2   How would you advertise each product? Be creative!

B **Discuss your answers with a partner.**

Reading Skill
Making Inferences

> Information in a reading passage is not always stated directly. Sometimes a reader has to infer (make guesses about) events or a writer's opinion, using the information that is available in the reading.

A **Skim the first paragraph of the passage on the next page. Make inferences to answer the following questions.**

    1   What do you think the main topic of the passage is?

       a advertisements that no one liked

       b famous commercials and slogans

       c advertisements that caused problems

    2   The two examples in the passage were mostly (positive / negative) experiences for the companies.

B **Skim the remaining paragraphs. Make inferences to answer the following questions.**

    1   American Apparel was (happy / unhappy) about Nancy Upton winning the contest.

    2   People felt bigger women were treated (well / badly) by the fashion industry.

    3   Some people did not like the Chevrolet Tahoe because of its (price / size).

C **Now read the entire passage carefully. Then answer the questions on page 132.**

Brand Engagement Gone Wrong

*Take a walk down the street and count the number of advertisements you see. With so many brands and companies competing for your attention, advertisers have to work harder than ever. One popular method of engaging **consumers** is by holding competitions where consumers come up with their own commercials or **slogans**. These have proven to be*
5 *successful, and do increase the number of people who come into contact with the brand. But allowing strangers to be active in a brand's identity can lead to great problems. Here are two cases of advertising gone wrong.*

Not a Model Spokesperson

When fashion brand American Apparel introduced its
10 new range of plus-sized[1] clothing, the company held a contest to find new models. In the contest, women could **submit** photos of themselves that showed off how nice the company's clothes look on larger women. But when the company advertised that it was looking for "the next
15 BIG thing," some women were offended because they thought the company was being disrespectful to women. An American actress called Nancy Upton decided to enter the contest to show the world how **insensitive** she thought American Apparel was.

Nancy took photos of herself in poses that **made fun of** the contest. She wore American
20 Apparel clothes and copied the style of their ads, but also ate fattening food, like burgers, in the photos. The photos became an Internet hit and she won the popular vote. While American Apparel did not recognize Nancy as the winner, her photos started a big discussion about how bigger women were treated in fashion, and Nancy became a hero to many.

Crashing the Commercial

25 Car manufacturer Chevrolet thought they had a good idea: organize a contest where people could create their own commercials for Chevrolet's newest and biggest vehicle, the Tahoe. The company **supplied** video and sound clips, and people could use computers to mix
30 them and add their own text. The contest accomplished its goal of promoting the Tahoe, as more than 30,000 videos were made.

While many entries focused on the best features of the truck, a few were less **flattering**; they pointed out
35 that the Tahoe was bad for the environment and that owning a big vehicle can sometimes lead to unsafe driving. Unfortunately, the negative videos spread fast, and Chevy got as much bad **publicity** as it did good publicity.

---

[1] Clothing for women in sizes larger than extra-large is said to be **plus-size**.

Reading Comprehension

Check Your Understanding

A Read the following sentences. Check (✔) true (*T*) or false (*F*).

		T	F
1	Companies usually avoid holding contests.		
2	A company cannot control who enters a contest, but they can control who wins.		
3	Nancy Upton did not enter the contest because she thought it was offensive to women.		
4	The few negative videos of the Tahoe were watched by many people.		
5	The contests were unsuccessful because they were not popular enough.		

B Which contest does each of the following sentences describe? Check (✔) American Apparel (*A*) or Chevrolet (*C*).

		A	C
1	Consumers thought the brand was hurting people's feelings.		
2	The contest earned the company both positive and negative publicity.		
3	People entered the contest because they did not approve of the product.		
4	The contest involved people sending photos of themselves using the product.		
5	Consumers could vote for the winner.		

Critical Thinking

C Discuss the following questions with a partner.

1 Do you think Nancy Upton deserved to win the contest? Why, or why not?

2 How can a company control its image in contests and other events?

Vocabulary Comprehension

Definitions

A Match each word or phrase with its definition. The words in blue are from the passage.

1 _____ consumer   **a** to give to somebody for their approval

2 _____ slogan   **b** a phrase that gets buyers' attention

3 _____ submit   **c** to say something to make a product or person look or feel good

4 _____ insensitive   **d** not noticing or caring about another person's feelings

5 _____ make fun of   **e** someone who uses a product

6 _____ publicity   **f** to provide something that is wanted or needed

7 _____ flatter   **g** to say something that hurts or upsets someone

8 _____ supply   **h** news to make a product or event popular

B Complete the following sentences using the words in blue from A. You might have to change the form of the word.

1 Getting mentioned in the newspaper is a good example of

_____ .

2 That new dress looks great on you. It's really _____!

3 Please don't _____ my brother's hair. He's very _____ about how he looks.

4 _____ voted for Nike's "Just Do It" as one of last century's most famous _____ .

A Use a dictionary to complete the chart with the correct noun, verb, and adjective forms. Compare your answers with a partner.

Verb	Adjective	Noun
1 offend	offending/offensive	offense
2	favored/favorite	
3		experience
4	imaginative	
5 scare		
6 concern		
7	suggestive	
8 support		

B Complete these advertisements with the correct word from the chart.

Shy? Lacking confidence? If the idea of speaking in public **(1)**_____ you, our program will change your life. With **(2)**_____ coaches who will **(3)**_____ you every step of the way, you'll soon overcome your fear.

Here's a(n) **(4)**_____ for people who **(5)**_____ the finer things in life—why not try our tailor-made luxury holidays? Sleep in a 5-star tent in Kenya. Swim in marble pools in Morocco. Go on a food tour of Tokyo. The only limit is your **(6)**_____ .

If bad breath is your **(7)**_____ , chew on our new Minty Bits. Try the freshest sweets in town, guaranteed to get rid of **(8)**_____ smells!

Real Life Skill

Advertising and Psychology

Many advertisements try to engage or "talk to" people's feelings and emotions—like fear and love—to persuade us that we need a product. They use certain words and images to produce reactions in us. For example, a company selling blankets can show images of puppies and use words like *warm* or *cuddly*.

A Read the following descriptions of commercials. Match each to the correct advertising message.

> **a** A woman is driving a car with her two small children in the backseat. Suddenly, another car turns in front of her. The mother hits the brakes, and her car immediately stops. The children are laughing and smiling.
>
> **b** A group of college-age friends are relaxing at the beach. All of a sudden, the sky turns gray and it starts to rain heavily. The friends get cans of soda from their cooler, and an invisible umbrella forms above them. They stay dry as they continue drinking soda.
>
> **c** An older couple are watching the sunrise from a cruise ship. Then, they are seen playing golf. Lastly, they are eating dinner in a beautiful restaurant. The watches on their wrists are clearly seen the whole time.

1 _____ This product will help you have fun.

2 _____ This product will show people you are rich.

3 _____ This product will keep you safe.

B Read the following slogans. With a partner, discuss what the advertising message of each slogan is.

1 The world's most beautiful women use SoftSilk Shampoo.

2 Drink Crystal Water. Cleaner, purer, safer.

3 Where is your child? You'll always know with Saftel cell phone.

C Now choose one of the three commercials in **A** and write a slogan for the product.

Motivational Tip: Review your reading fluency progress. Refer to the reading rate and reading comprehension charts at the end of the book. How would you evaluate your progress? Are your scores gradually going up? Use these charts to evaluate the progress you are making. What goals can you set for yourself as you continue to the next unit?

What do you think?

1 Some people think advertising has turned us into a greedier society. Do you agree? Why, or why not?

2 Should companies be allowed to advertise to children? Why, or why not?

3 Advertising has changed a lot over the last few decades. How do you think it will change in the next 10 or 20 years?

Food and the Environment

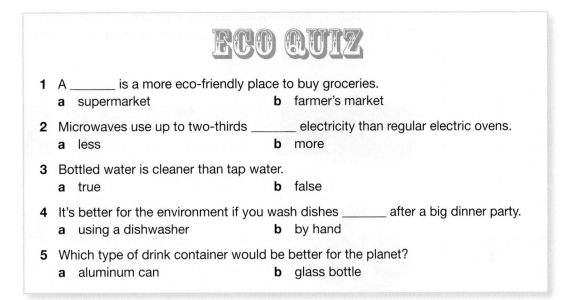

ECO QUIZ

1 A _____ is a more eco-friendly place to buy groceries.
  a supermarket   **b** farmer's market

2 Microwaves use up to two-thirds _____ electricity than regular electric ovens.
  a less   **b** more

3 Bottled water is cleaner than tap water.
  a true   **b** false

4 It's better for the environment if you wash dishes _____ after a big dinner party.
  a using a dishwasher   **b** by hand

5 Which type of drink container would be better for the planet?
  a aluminum can   **b** glass bottle

Getting Ready

A Complete the quiz above, then discuss your answers with a partner.

B Check your answers below. How many did you get correct?
  1 b: A farmer's market is more likely to sell foods that are grown in the area, while a supermarket normally sells foods that have traveled thousands of kilometers. Buying local foods saves fuel and reduces pollution caused by transportation.
  2 a: A microwave uses 50–65 percent less energy to heat food than regular ovens. This is because it works faster and focuses energy directly on the food, as compared to heating the surrounding air like in an oven.
  3 b: In many countries, tap water has to meet higher standards than bottled water. So bottled water is not necessarily cleaner!
  4 a: If you have many things to wash, use a dishwasher. It uses half the energy, one-sixth of the water, and less soap compared to washing everything by hand.
  5 a: Making aluminum cans requires less energy than making glass bottles. They're also more commonly recycled and are usually made from 40 percent recycled aluminum.

Motivational Tip: Reading in English is important. Being able to read well in English will help you to achieve sucess in and out of the classroom. As you make progress in this chapter, it will help you as you set and reach your goals outside of the classroom.

CHAPTER 1 Engineering a Better Burger

Before You Read
A Healthy Meal

A Think about answers to the following questions.

1 Which would you rather eat from each pair of foods below? Why?

2 Which are natural foods and which are processed? Which do you think is healthier? Why?

OR

OR

B Discuss your answers with a partner.

Reading Skill
Distinguishing between Main and Supporting Ideas

Every paragraph has a main idea, with supporting ideas that explain the main idea. The main idea is usually in the beginning of the paragraph—but not always! By knowing the difference between main and supporting ideas, you can understand the purpose of a passage more clearly.

A Skim each paragraph in the passage on the next page. Circle the sentence that describes the main idea of each paragraph.

Paragraph 1
   a Most people on the planet are omnivores.
   b People are eating more meat.

Paragraph 2
   a Raising animals for meat has changed the world for the worse.
   b Methane and carbon dioxide are greenhouse gasses.

Paragraph 3
   a Scientists are coming up with new ways to produce meat.
   b Stem cells can be used to create beef in a laboratory.

B Read paragraph 4. Write the main idea and one supporting idea.

Paragraph 4
Main idea: _____
Supporting idea: _____

C Now read the entire passage carefully. Then answer the questions on page 138.

Engineering a Better Burger

1 Humans have traditionally been omnivores, with a diet of both meat and vegetables. But lately it seems we've become a society of meat eaters. According to the United Nation's Food and Agriculture Organization (FAO), global demand for meat has increased over 500 percent in the past 50 years. Two things explain this: the Earth's population is rising rapidly, and people with higher
5 incomes tend to consume more meat. With the population expected to reach nine billion people around 2050, and with developing countries getting richer, this trend won't stop any time soon.

2 If meat production rises to match demand, the **consequences** could be **devastating** for the planet. Thirty percent of Earth's entire land surface—a massive 70 percent of all land available for agricultural use—is used for raising livestock. And more land is required each year as farmers
10 **struggle** to meet the rising demand, which comes at the cost of rain forests and other valuable land. Reports by FAO show that meat production is responsible for 70 percent of the Amazon deforestation in South America. Large factory farms are also big consumers of energy and cause a lot of pollution. It's clear that our hunger for meat, and the way we produce it, is not **sustainable** in the long run.

3 15 Fortunately, food scientists have been **anticipating** this need for change. They are working on some interesting **alternatives** to current methods of meat production. A group of Dutch scientists are engineering meats that can be grown in laboratories. This involves using cells taken from cows to grow "muscle" that can be mixed with other things to make beef. They say that this process could reduce the amount of energy and land needed to raise cattle by about 40 percent.
20 Other scientists from the United States and China are working to create "meaty" flavors from mushrooms, which could be used to flavor foods. They feel people can detect **chemical** flavors, and that natural flavors are better for the body.

4 For now, lab-grown meat is not a threat to traditional farming. Although scientists say that their beef could be ready for testing (and eating) soon, large-scale manufacturing won't be possible for
25 another ten years. It's far too expensive to develop in large quantities—the Dutch team will spend over $200,000 making enough meat for one burger—and not everyone will be **keen** on the idea of eating lab-grown meat. While the general public isn't quite ready to accept "fake" meat, the day will come when we may not have a choice.

Reading Comprehension

Check Your Understanding

A Read the following sentences. Check (✓) true (*T*) or false (*F*).

	T	F
1 People with more money usually eat less meat.		
2 Most of Earth's usable land goes to livestock farming.		
3 Some scientists are trying to make mushrooms taste like meat.		
4 Lab-grown meat costs more than normal meat.		
5 Lab-grown meat will be sold in supermarkets very soon.		

B Complete the following summary with words or phrases from the passage.

Global demand for meat has risen by **(1)**_____ in the last 50 years, partly because the population has grown, and also because people are generally getting **(2)**_____. This rising demand has a huge effect on the environment. Livestock farms already occupy **(3)**_____ of all agricultural land, and **(4)**_____ are being destroyed to create even more land for this purpose. Raising large numbers of livestock also consumes a lot of **(5)**_____ and causes a lot of **(6)**_____. But science may have a solution. Some scientists are trying to make meat in a **(7)**_____ by taking **(8)**_____ from cows to grow **(9)**_____. However, it will take at least ten years to produce meat in large quantities, because it is **(10)**_____ to manufacture. Other scientists are creating "meaty" flavors from **(11)**_____; they believe these **(12)**_____ flavors taste better and are healthier. In the end, though, a lot depends on whether the public can accept these meat alternatives.

Critical Thinking

C Discuss the following questions with a partner.

1 Would you rather eat foods that are created in a lab or grown naturally? Why?

2 Can you think of any meat alternatives that are already available to the public?

Vocabulary Comprehension

Odd Word Out

A Circle the word or phrase that does not belong in each group. The words in blue are from the passage.

1	struggle	relax	rest	calm down
2	ask	consequence	demand	request
3	attracting	polluting	damaging	devastating
4	anticipation	feeling	emotion	mood
5	limitation	choice	alternative	option
6	support	keep up	limit	sustain
7	interested	curious	keen	disgusted
8	chemical	fake	manufactured	natural

B Complete the following sentences with the words in blue from **A**. You might have to change the form of the words.

1 He does not have enough customers to _____ his business.
2 Many people _____ to lose weight. The problem is they are _____ to diet and exercise but never really follow through.
3 Cycling is a good _____ to driving.
4 The boxer _____ his opponent's punch and moved out of the way.

A Look at some examples of where adverbs are placed in a sentence.

Many adverbs can be placed either before or after the verb they describe.

> She spoke *confidently* about her new project.
> She *confidently* spoke about her new project.

Some adverbs appear at the very beginning of a sentence and describe the entire sentence. Some adverbs describe a clause within the sentence.

> *Suddenly*, it started raining, but *luckily* I had my umbrella with me.

Sometimes adverbs appear at the end of a sentence. If a sentence has more than one verb, we avoid putting the adverb at the end.

> ✗ The boys sang the songs that they had prepared in class *loudly*.
> ✓ The boys *loudly* sang the songs that they had prepared in class.

Vocabulary Skill
Adverbs

In this chapter, we saw the words *traditionally* and *easily*. These are examples of adverbs. Adverbs can be used to describe verbs in a sentence; they tell us how something is done. An adverb usually appears right before or after the verb it describes, but it can also appear at the beginning or the end of a sentence.

B Write the adverb form of these adjectives.

Adjective	Adverb	Adjective	Adverb
1 tradition		6 sincere	
2 aggressive		7 passionate	
3 virtual		8 persuasive	
4 previous		9 loyal	
5 essential		10 natural	

C Read the sentences below. (Circle) the adverb. Then, underline the word, phrase, clause, or sentence that the adverb describes.

1 The lion in the cage roared aggressively.
2 Frankly, I'm not bothered about what he thinks.
3 The president argued for lower taxes very persuasively.
4 Many dogs follow their owner loyally and listen to their commands.
5 The James family traditionally go to France for Christmas.

CHAPTER 2 Is Your Diet Destroying the Environment?

Before You Read
Problems from Food

A Think about answers to the following questions.

1 How do foods get from the farm to our table? Number the images (1-5) based on the stages in the process.

2 What problems to the Earth could each stage cause?

B Discuss your answers with a partner.

Reading Skill
Understanding Cause and Effect

> Sometimes a reading is organized around the causes and effects of a problem or situation. Understanding these cause and effect relationships will help you to understand the author's main idea.

A The following sentences are from the passage on the next page. Write the cause and the effect.

1 Some adopt a vegetarian diet as the ethical alternative to eating meat, because they believe killing animals is wrong.
   Cause _some people believe killing animals is wrong_
   Effect _these people become vegetarian_

2 Animals such as cows, pigs, and sheep release methane—a greenhouse gas that causes global warming—when they pass wind.
   Cause _____
   Effect _____

3 A vegan diet may deprive us of vitamins and minerals that are essential to our health.
   Cause _____
   Effect _____

B Read the entire passage carefully. Then answer the questions on page 142.

Is Your Diet Destroying the Environment?

1 People become vegetarian for different reasons. Some **adopt** a vegetarian diet as the **ethical** alternative to eating meat, because they believe killing animals is wrong. People who are concerned about their health see it as a good way to keep slim and lower their risk of various diseases. Lately, more people are replacing meat with vegetables because of the **vital** role this plays in protecting
5 the environment.

2 Researchers from the Union of Concerned Scientists in the U.S. released a report on the **impact** of consumer behavior on the environment. Their study showed that meat consumption is one of the main ways that humans can damage the environment, second only to the use of motor vehicles.

3 But how will **modifying** our diets make a difference? We can compare the amount of resources
10 needed to produce meat and crops[1]. For example, we need almost 20,000 liters of water to produce a kilogram of beef, whereas only 150 liters of water is needed to produce a kilogram of wheat. Similarly, one hectare (or 10,000 square meters) of farmland that is used for raising livestock produces about 227 kilograms of beef, but the same amount of farmland can produce 13,600 kilograms of carrots, 18,000 kilograms of potatoes, or 22,700 kilograms of tomatoes. It's clear that
15 we can make more efficient use of land and water if we produce crops instead of meat.

4 Raising livestock also contributes to rising global temperatures. Animals such as cows, pigs, and sheep release methane—a greenhouse gas that causes global warming—when they pass wind, with one cow producing an **estimated** 500 liters of methane each day. A 2006 report by the Food and Agriculture Organization (FAO) says that livestock farming **accounts for** 37 percent
20 of all methane production, and warns that methane may have a more damaging effect on the atmosphere than carbon dioxide.

5 There is growing support for vegetarianism. For example, schools across England and the U.S. hold "Meat Free Mondays" to show students how easy it is to eat less meat. Some people go one step further and eat a vegan diet, which excludes all animal products such as cheese, eggs, and milk.
25 However, some nutritionists believe that a vegan diet may **deprive** us of vitamins and minerals that are essential to our health.

6 One does not have to become vegan or fully vegetarian to help save the environment. Whether it's just being vegetarian for one day a week—or just eating less meat—a small effort on our part can go a long way.

---

[1] **Crops** are plants such as wheat and potatoes that are grown in large amounts for food.

Reading Comprehension
Check Your Understanding

A Choose the correct answers for the following questions.

1 Which is NOT mentioned as a reason people become vegetarian?
   a They think meat is too expensive.
   b They think eating meat is morally wrong.
   c They think eating meat is bad for health.

2 What do you think "Meat Free Mondays" is about?
   a Meat is free for students on Mondays.
   b Students try not to eat meat on Mondays.
   c Students take classes on environmental issues.

3 What does *go one step further* in lines 23—24 mean?
   a travel more
   b learn more
   c do more

B Which amount is <u>larger</u>? (Circle) the correct item in each pair.

1 the damage done to the environment by (eating meat / driving)
2 the amount of global warming caused by (methane gas / carbon dioxide)
3 the water needed to produce a kilogram of (meat / vegetables)
4 the amount of (meat / vegetables) you can produce on a piece of land
5 the vitamins in a (vegan / vegetarian) diet

Critical Thinking

C Discuss the following questions with a partner.

1 Can you think of any disadvantages of being vegetarian?
2 Do you agree with the final sentence of the passage—that a small effort can go a long way?

Vocabulary Comprehension
Definitions

A Choose the best answer. The words in blue are from the passage.

1 When you adopt something, you _____ it.
   a accept   b reject

2 Something that is ethical is seen as _____ .
   a right   b wrong

3 Which would account for traffic accidents?
   a more traffic lights   b careless driving

4 _____ is vital to your health.
   a Exercising   b Smoking

5 If something has an impact on your life, it _____ .
   a has changed you greatly   b means very little to you

6 If you estimate a number, you think of an _____ .
   a exact number, like 338   b approximately correct number, like 300

7 When you modify something, you change it _____ .
   a slightly   **b** completely

8 A man deprived of food is _____ .
   a fat   **b** thin

B **Answer the following questions, then discuss your answers with a partner. The words in blue are from the passage.**

1 What's the best way to adopt good habits?
2 Who in your family has had the biggest impact on your life?
3 How would you define something as ethical or unethical?
4 What is a vital part of learning a new language?

A **Complete the following chart, then write the word next to the correct definition. Use your dictionary to help you.**

Vocabulary Skill
The Root Word *vit*/*viv*

Word	Part of speech	Word	Part of speech
vitamin		vivid	
survive		revive	
vivacious			

1 _____: to make something active and healthy again
2 _____: substances in food that keep you healthy
3 _____: very clear and detailed
4 _____: to continue to live
5 _____: very lively and energetic

In this chapter, you learned the adjective *vital*, a word made by combining the root word *vit*, meaning *life*, with the suffix *-al*, meaning *like* or relating to. *Vit*, also sometimes written as *viv*, can be combined with other prefixes and suffixes to form many words in English.

B **Complete each sentence using a word from A. You might have to change the form of the word.**

1 The couple was in a serious car accident, but luckily they _____ .
2 Which has more _____ C: an orange, or a glass of orange juice?
3 I have very _____ memories of growing up in Italy.
4 You look tired. Maybe drinking some coffee will help to _____ you.
5 Sandra is such a _____ and outgoing woman that everyone in the office likes her.

C **Now come up with two sentences of your own using words from the chart. Share your sentences with a partner.**

Motivational Tip: Too challenging or too easy? Challenging reading provides the opportunity to use effective reading strategies. Easier reading provides the opportunity to practice reading fluency. In order to improve your reading abilities, you will need a combination of both.

Real Life Skill
Understanding Units of Measure

Most of the world uses the metric system to measure things like length and weight. Some countries, though, use non-metric measures, or a combination of both. The metric system uses prefixes to indicate the size of the number. The most common prefixes are *milli* (0.001), *centi* (0.01), and *kilo* (1,000). For example, one kilometer is equal to 1,000 meters, while one meter is equal to 100 centimeters.

A Review the comparisons in the chart. What does each measure? Complete the chart using the words from the box below. One word is used twice.

~~weight~~	temperature	distance
volume	length	area

Measures	Non-metric vs. Metric
weight	1 pound (lb) = 453.6 grams
	1 foot (ft) = 0.3 meters (m)
	1 inch (in) = 2.5 cm
	1 gallon = 4.5 liters (l)
	1 mile = 1.6 kilometers (km) = 1600 meters (m)
	32 Fahrenheit (°F) = 0 Celsius (°C) To convert Celsius to Fahrenheit: [number in Celsius] x 1.8, add 32.
	1 hectare = 10,000 square meters (m²) = about 2.5 acres

B Use the correct form of the words below to compare each set of measurements. Not all the words will be used.

big cold heavy hot less light long more short small

1 One pound is ___lighter___ than one kilogram.
2 One inch is _____ than one centimeter.
3 One gallon contains _____ liquid than one liter.
4 One kilometer is _____ than one mile.
5 50° F is _____ than 50°C.
6 One hectare is _____ than one acre.

What do you think?

1 Would you change your eating habits to help the environment? Why, or why not?
2 How do you think our diet will change 10 or 20 years from now? Why?
3 Do you think everyone in the world should use the same measurement system? Why do you think some people use the metric system and others use a non-metric system?

Living for the Future 12

Are you a friend of the environment?

	always	sometimes	never
1 I turn off lights when I leave the room.	☐	☐	☐
2 I recycle paper, or write on the reverse side of the page.	☐	☐	☐
3 I recycle aluminum cans and plastic drink bottles.	☐	☐	☐
4 I use public transportation such as buses or trains.	☐	☐	☐
5 I buy used or recycled products.	☐	☐	☐
6 I take short showers and use water carefully.	☐	☐	☐
7 I eat more vegetables than meat.	☐	☐	☐
8 I avoid buying products with wasteful packaging.	☐	☐	☐

Getting Ready

A Complete the survey above by checking (✔) the boxes that apply to you.

B Compare your results to the answers below. How did you do? Can you think of more ways to be environmentally friendly?

> **If you answered mostly...**
>
> **always:** You look for ways to use less and recycle more, even if it requires more effort or time. Congratulations for being a true friend of the environment!
>
> **sometimes:** It's awesome that you're thinking about the future! Keep doing what you're doing, and think of more ways you can help out.
>
> **never:** Don't worry if you've never done these things before—it's not too late to start! Take small steps, like turning off electronics when you're not using them, or taking showers instead of baths.

CHAPTER 1 Clean Up Australia, Clean Up the World

Before You Read
How Clean Is Your City?

A Think about answers to the following questions.

1 Do you think your city is clean or dirty? Why do you think so?
2 Why are some cities cleaner than others? What can people do to make their cities cleaner?
3 What are some kinds of volunteer work that people do to help the environment?

B Discuss your answers with a partner.

Reading Skill
Scanning for Names and Numbers

> Key information in a passage often contains numbers, dates, or names of people, places, and events. Sometimes numbers are written as digits (1, 2, 3) and sometimes as words (one, two, three).

A Read the following questions. (Circle) the type of information you need to scan for.

1 When did Ian Kiernan organize his first Clean Up event?   date   name   number
   Answer: _____
2 How many people took part in the first Clean Up Australia?   date   name   number
   Answer: _____
3 Which organization helped Kiernan organize Clean Up the World?   date   name   number
   Answer: _____
4 How many countries took part in the first Clean Up the World?   date   name   number
   Answer: _____
5 What program helps people reuse and recycle cell phones?   date   name   number
   Answer: _____

B Now scan the passage on the next page and answer the questions in A.

C Read the entire passage carefully. Then answer the questions on page 148.

> **Motivational Tip: Reevaluate the questions.** Review each of your responses on the comprehension questions in this unit. For the items you got correct, identify why you got them correct. For the items you got incorrect, identify reasons why you missed those questions. When you review questions you missed, you can identify mistakes and learn from them.

Clean Up Australia, Clean Up the World

http://www.asrinfo.heinle.com/cleanup

Ian Kiernan was taking part in an around-the-world sailing race in 1987 when he noticed an **alarming** amount of garbage in the oceans. Returning home to Australia, Kiernan felt he had to do something about it.

5   He started close to home by organizing a community event in 1989 called Clean Up Sydney Harbour. To his surprise, more than 40,000 **volunteers** came out to clear away garbage. Encouraged by this success, Kiernan decided to make the clean-up a national event 10   the following year. It took off—across Australia, an estimated 300,000 people spent the day working to improve their local environment.

Clean Up Australia Day has been held annually since then, growing bigger every year. In 1993, Kiernan started 15   an even more **ambitious** program. With the help of the United Nations Environment Program, he **launched** Clean Up the World to support communities around the world in cleaning up and conserving the environment. In its first year, more than 30 million people in 80 countries 20   participated. Clean Up the World now falls on the third weekend of September every year, and has grown more popular as the years go by.

Today, Clean Up Australia Day welcomes more than half a million volunteers who help to clear thousands of tons of garbage from beaches, parks, streets, and waterways. They pick up 25   used cigarettes, glass and plastic bottles, plastic bags, and thousands of snack food wrappers.

In recent years Kiernan says that there has been an increase in harmful electronic **waste**—such as computers and cell phones—and that e-waste is **accumulating** faster than other trash. E-waste sometimes makes up 70 percent of the overall waste found in landfills, according to Global Futures Foundation. Kiernan feels that companies need to take more responsibility for the 30   clean-up and recycling of their products, since chemicals from e-waste can cause health problems if they leak into the ground or into the water supply. To help deal with e-waste, Kiernan started a program called Clean Up Mobile Phones to collect used cell phones for reuse and recycling.

Ian saw a problem that needed fixing, and he chose to take action. By starting Clean Up Australia Day, he raised awareness of how we treat our Earth. What's more, he **united** millions 35   of people in their goal to make the world a cleaner place. Through **persistence** and hard work, Ian has shown that anyone who puts their mind to it can make a difference.

Reading Comprehension
Check Your Understanding

A Choose the correct answer for the following questions.

1 What is another possible title for this passage?
   a The Dangers of Electronic Waste
   b Small Ideas, Big Impact
   c Who Is Ian Kiernan?

2 Which event is no longer running?
   a Clean Up Sydney Harbour
   b Clean Up Australia
   c Clean Up The World

3 Which is NOT true about e-waste?
   a It is dangerous to people.
   b It has been a growing problem over the last few years.
   c Many companies have special programs to deal with it.

4 The purpose of the last paragraph is to show that _____.
   a even one person can make a difference to the world
   b lots of people want to help the environment
   c Ian Kiernan should be rewarded for doing a good job

B Put these events in the correct order from 1–6.

___1___ Kiernan competed in international sailing races.

_____ Kiernan worked with the United Nations to start an international program.

_____ Forty thousand people picked up garbage in Sydney.

_____ Kiernan became concerned about environmental problems.

_____ Kiernan began focusing on recycling old computers and cell phones.

_____ People across Australia worked to clean up garbage.

Critical Thinking

C Discuss the following questions with a partner.

1 Would a clean-up day be popular in your country? Why, or why not?
2 Where do you think all the trash goes after being collected?

Vocabulary Comprehension
Words in Context

A Choose the best answer. The words in blue are from the passage.

1 The baby was alarmed by the _____ noise.
   a soft   b loud

2 Volunteers _____ for the work they do.
   a get paid   b don't receive pay

3 When you start an ambitious project, it will _____.
   a take a lot of time and effort   b be very easy to finish

4 If you launch something, you _____ it.
   a start   b stop

5 Waste is generally _____ .

    a kept on a computer   **b** thrown into a trash can

6 When money accumulates, it is earned _____ .

    a over a long period of time   **b** all at once

7 An army that is united is usually _____ .

    a weaker   **b** stronger

8 A person who is persistent is likely to be _____ .

    a hardworking   **b** lazy

B **Answer the following questions, then discuss your answers with a partner. The words in blue are from the passage.**

1 Do you like to accumulate things, or throw things away?

2 Name a volunteer organization that does important work in your country.

3 What is your ambition in life? How will you accomplish it?

4 Is persistence or talent more important for success? Why do you think so?

A **Read the flyer below and (circle) all of the *re-* words you find.**

Vocabulary Skill
The Prefix *re-*

> In this chapter, you saw the verb *recycle*, a word made by combining the prefix *re-*, meaning *again or back/return*, with the verb *cycle*, meaning *to happen again*.
> *Re-* can be combined with nouns, verbs, adjectives, and root words to form many words in English.

Recycle more with Sunrise Collection Services!

Can you recall how much you spent last month on your electricity bill? Now you can save the planet AND reduce your monthly bills by separating plastic, tin, aluminum, and paper from your weekly trash. Every kilogram of trash you return is a dollar off your bill. You will get a refund for the total amount at the end of the year.

Visit our brand new website to find out more. You can now do more online, such as renew your SunRise Collection Club membership, review and adjust price plans for waste collection services, and contact us with questions or comments.

B **Match each of the *re-* words from A with the definitions below.**

1 _____ : to begin or take up again

2 _____ : to make something smaller

3 _____ : to use a waste item again

4 _____ : money that is given back

5 _____ : to give back something

6 _____ : to look something over

7 _____ : to remember or hear again

C **Are there any other words beginning with *re-* that you can add to this list? What do they mean? Discuss your answers with a partner.**

Before You Read
Our Natural Resources

A **Answer the following questions.**

1 How many natural resources can you list?
water, oil,

2 Which of these resources does your country have plenty of? (Circle) them. Which resources are likely to run out in the future and be a problem?

B **Discuss your answers with a partner.**

Reading Skill
Skimming to Assess a Passage

> Skimming can help you decide whether a reading contains the information that you are looking for. If it does contain useful information, then you can read it again more slowly.

A **Imagine that you need to choose an essay topic on the environment. Skim the article on the next page and check (✔) the topics that it would help you with.**

1 ☐ Animals in the Rain Forest

2 ☐ Why We Need Fresh Water

3 ☐ Government Laws on Natural Resources

4 ☐ Turning Sea Water into Fresh Water

5 ☐ The Importance of the Amazon

6 ☐ Natural Resources: Running Out?

B **Skim the article again and write the correct paragraph number for each main idea.**

1 _____ We all need to contribute to saving our environment.
2 _____ Our food supply is linked to the amount of fresh water available.
3 _____ Rain forests are being destroyed at an alarming rate.
4 _____ Water is important for every form of life.
5 _____ The Earth's rising population is threatening natural resources.

C **Now read the entire passage carefully. Then answer the questions on page 152.**

Resources for the Future

1 We are a planet of seven billion people, and this number is growing by about 370,000 people every day. This is putting a huge **strain** on the planet's natural resources. For many governments and environmental organizations, the race is on to **drastically** reduce our consumption of resources before they run out.

2 Water is one of our most precious resources. Our quality of life, as well as life itself, depends on the **availability** of clean, fresh water. It is the most widely used resource in industry, and plays a major role in energy production. Although 70 percent of the world is covered in water, only 2.5 percent of that is fresh water, and less than one percent of that fresh water is readily available to us. Yet we often overestimate how much water we have, and reduce it further through pollution or inefficient use.

3 Some 92 percent of all fresh water used annually is dedicated to growing plants and raising animals for food. This means that if water runs out, our food supply might follow. In India, it is estimated that future water **shortages** could reduce grain harvests by 25 percent. In a country where the population **exceeds** 1.2 billion people and is growing rapidly every year, this is a huge concern. India, like many developing countries, is already struggling to provide for its population. While most people in developed countries can get water at the turn of a tap, nearly four billion people elsewhere **lack** access to safe water, according to a 2012 United Nations' World Water Development Report.

4 Rain forests are another **endangered** resource. They once covered 14 percent of the Earth's land surface, but this has shrunk to only six percent. Every second, an area of rain forest the size of a football field is destroyed—at this rate, rain forests will disappear completely in less than 40 years. All rain forests are important, but it would be a disaster if the Amazon rain forest was gone. Often called the "Lungs of the Planet," the Amazon stretches across a large portion of South America. It is so big that it produces 20 percent of the Earth's oxygen, and is home to more than half of the world's estimated ten million species of plants and animals.

5 Governments around the world have laws to help protect and conserve these precious resources. But, no matter how many rules there are, it is ultimately individuals who must help the planet to **sustain** itself. Changing our lifestyle and limiting our use of natural resources is the only way to ensure a better future for our children, and our children's children.

Reading Comprehension
Check Your Understanding

A **Choose the correct answers for the following questions.**

1 What does the writer mean when he says *people in developed countries can get water at the turn of a tap* in line 20?

   a Water is easily available to people in developed countries.

   b People in developing countries do not have taps.

   c People in developed countries waste more water.

2 The writer uses India as an example of a country that _____.

   a pollutes and wastes water

   b depends on water to grow food

   c has access to lots of clean water

3 Why does the author discuss *our children's children* in the last line?

   a to say people who have children cause the most problems

   b to compare the lifestyle of children and adults

   c to suggest our actions affect the world beyond a few years

B **Read the following sentences. Check (✔) if the sentence is true for water (*W*) or rain forests (*R*).**

	W	R
1 A large amount of this resource is not easily available.		
2 This natural resource helps provide the air we breathe.		
3 Population growth is one reason this is under threat.		
4 Losing this will have a big impact on the world.		
5 Governments have laws to protect this natural resource.		
6 This might be completely gone in four decades.		

Critical Thinking

C **Answer the following questions, then discuss your answers with a partner.**

1 Have you ever been in a situation where there was no clean water? How long did you not have water for? What did you do?

2 Can you think of any natural resources that will never run out? Explain your answer.

Vocabulary Comprehension
Odd Word Out

A (Circle) **the word or phrase that does not belong in each group. The words in blue are from the passage.**

1 strain	ease	difficulty	stress
2 extremely	greatly	suddenly	drastically
3 opportunity	availability	busy	possibility
4 lack	shortage	exceed	missing
5 forever	everlasting	endangered	permanent
6 sustain	discontinue	keep going	maintain

B Complete the following sentences with the words in blue from **A**. You might have to change the form of the word.

1 What kind of situations can put a(n) _____ on a relationship?
2 The town has changed _____ since the last time I visited.
3 The tiger is a(n) _____ animal. There aren't many left in the wild.
4 It's easy to launch a business but it's difficult to _____ it.

A The following chart contains common nouns, verbs, and adjectives that use the prefixes *over* and *under*. Check (✔) the prefix that can be combined with each word; sometimes both prefixes can be used. You may use a dictionary to help you.

Word	over	under	Word	over	under
1 weight			**6** paid		
2 state			**7** mine		
3 heated			**8** sized		
4 achieve			**9** dose		
5 way			**10** flow		

Vocabulary Skill
The Prefixes *over* and *under*

In the passage you read the word *overestimate*, meaning *to think there is more than what is available*. The opposite of this would be *underestimate*. The two prefixes *over* and *under* can be added to nouns, verbs, and adjectives.

B Complete the following movie review with the correct form of the words from **A**.

Movie Review

Opening this week is *Eat Less/Live More*, a movie that follows the journey of Jacob Harris from **(1)** _____ achiever to environmental hero. At the start of the movie, Jacob is 30 kilograms **(2)** _____ weight and miserable in his **(3)** _____ paid job. When his car **(4)** _____ heats one hot summer day, he decides to walk to work. This inspires him to think of ways he can lose weight while living a more sustainable life. As his transformation gets **(5)** _____ way, the benefits turn out to be mental as much as physical, like in one hilarious scene where he stands up to a colleague who keeps trying to **(6)** _____ mine him. This movie has an **(7)** _____ stated style and an **(8)** _____ sized heart. **9/10**

Motivational Tip: More than the definition. After completing this vocabulary exercise, think about what it means to truly know a word. If you know a word, you know more than the definition. You know the context in which this word will appear, and what other words can be used near this word. I challenge you to think about more than just the definition of a word in order to improve your vocabullary skills.

Real Life Skill
Reading Numbers in Text

Different countries use different counting systems. Practice will help you get used to reading numbers in another language. Commas are used with large numbers to separate the thousands or between every three digits (e.g. 3,000,000).

A Look at the chart to see how numbers are written and spoken in English.

Written	Spoken
1,000	one thousand, a thousand, one K (kay)
1,500	one thousand five hundred, fifteen hundred
10,000	ten thousand
100,000	one hundred thousand, a hundred thousand
225,000	two hundred (and) twenty-five thousand
1,000,000	one million, a million
1,500,000	one million five hundred thousand, one point five million (1.5 million)

B Write the numbers for the following amounts. Remember to add commas.

1 _____ two million
2 _____ four million five hundred thousand
3 _____ four hundred fifty-five thousand
4 _____ seventeen hundred twenty-eight
5 _____ ten thousand seven hundred

C Read the following passage to yourself. Then read one paragraph aloud to a partner, and listen as your partner reads the second paragraph to you.

Cigarettes and the Environment

When you think about trash, you probably don't think about cigarette butts. With almost 4.5 trillion cigarettes being smoked worldwide each year, where are the butts (the unused ends of cigarettes) going? About 66 percent of butts don't go into trash cans, but litter our beaches and streets. During the 2007 Great Canadian Shoreline Cleanup, volunteers collected some 270,000 cigarette butts.

Making cigarettes also affects the environment. Farmers use wood fires to dry tobacco leaves, using over 11 million tons of wood each year. This means nearly 600 million trees are cut down every single year. In southern Africa alone, 200,000 hectares of forest are chopped down annually. To make things worse, manufacturing cigarettes creates lots of factory waste, reaching a high of 2,460 million kilograms in 1995. That's a lot of trash!

What do you think?

1 How can individual people preserve the environment?
2 Do you think volunteer activities are a good way to solve environmental problems? Explain your answer.
3 Whose responsibility is it to keep the ocean and land clean? Why?

Review Unit 4

In order to become a more fluent reader, remember to follow the six points of the ACTIVE approach—before, while, and after you read. See the inside front cover for more information on the ACTIVE approach.

Activate Prior Knowledge

Before you read, it's important to think about what you already know about the topic, and what you want to get out of the text.

A Look at the passage on the next page. Read the title and look at the photo. What do you think the article is about? What are *billboards*?

B Think more about the topic. What do you know about billboards? Where can you see them in your country? What products are advertised on them? Discuss with a partner.

Cultivate Vocabulary

As you read, you may come across unknown words. Remember, you don't need to understand all the words to understand the meaning of the passage. Skip the unknown words for now, or guess at their meaning and come back to them later. Note useful new vocabulary in your vocabulary notebook—see page 6 for more advice on vocabulary.

A Now read the first paragraph of the passage. (Circle) any words or phrases you don't know. Can you understand the rest of the paragraph even if you don't understand those items?

B Write the unknown words here. Without using a dictionary, try to guess their meanings. Use the words around the unknown word and any prefixes, suffixes, or word roots to help you.

New word/phrase	I think it means...

Think About Meaning

As you read, think about what you can infer, or "read between the lines," for example, about the author's intention, attitudes, and purpose for writing.

Read the opening paragraph again and discuss these questions with a partner.

• What do you think is the purpose of the reading? Why did the author write it?
• How do you think the author feels about billboards with advanced technology? Do you think he or she is in favor of it, or against it?
• Why does the author call the billboards *high-tech devices*? How are the billboards *high-tech*?

Increase Reading Fluency

To increase your reading fluency, it's important to monitor your own reading habits as you read. Look again at the tips on page 8. As you read, follow these tips.

Now read the whole passage *Billboards That Recognize You*. As you read, check your predictions from *Think About Meaning*.

BILLBOARDS THAT RECOGNIZE YOU

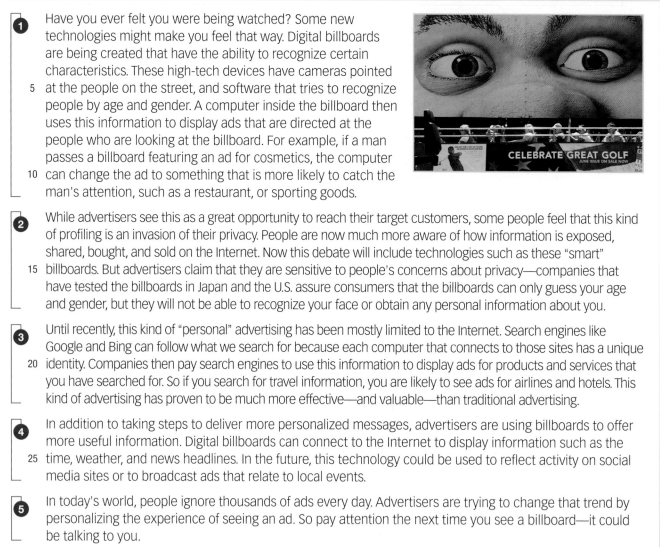

1 Have you ever felt you were being watched? Some new technologies might make you feel that way. Digital billboards are being created that have the ability to recognize certain characteristics. These high-tech devices have cameras pointed
5 at the people on the street, and software that tries to recognize people by age and gender. A computer inside the billboard then uses this information to display ads that are directed at the people who are looking at the billboard. For example, if a man passes a billboard featuring an ad for cosmetics, the computer
10 can change the ad to something that is more likely to catch the man's attention, such as a restaurant, or sporting goods.

2 While advertisers see this as a great opportunity to reach their target customers, some people feel that this kind of profiling is an invasion of their privacy. People are now much more aware of how information is exposed, shared, bought, and sold on the Internet. Now this debate will include technologies such as these "smart"
15 billboards. But advertisers claim that they are sensitive to people's concerns about privacy—companies that have tested the billboards in Japan and the U.S. assure consumers that the billboards can only guess your age and gender, but they will not be able to recognize your face or obtain any personal information about you.

3 Until recently, this kind of "personal" advertising has been mostly limited to the Internet. Search engines like Google and Bing can follow what we search for because each computer that connects to those sites has a unique
20 identity. Companies then pay search engines to use this information to display ads for products and services that you have searched for. So if you search for travel information, you are likely to see ads for airlines and hotels. This kind of advertising has proven to be much more effective—and valuable—than traditional advertising.

4 In addition to taking steps to deliver more personalized messages, advertisers are using billboards to offer more useful information. Digital billboards can connect to the Internet to display information such as the
25 time, weather, and news headlines. In the future, this technology could be used to reflect activity on social media sites or to broadcast ads that relate to local events.

5 In today's world, people ignore thousands of ads every day. Advertisers are trying to change that trend by personalizing the experience of seeing an ad. So pay attention the next time you see a billboard—it could be talking to you.

Verify Strategies

To build your reading fluency, it's important to be aware of how you use strategies to read, and to consider how successfully you are using them.

Use the questions in the *Self Check* on page 158 to think about your use of reading strategies.

Evaluate Progress

Evaluating your progress means thinking about how much you understood from the passage, and how fluently you were able to read the passage to get the information you needed.

Check how well you understood the passage by answering the following questions.

1 What is another possible title for the passage?
   a The Dangers of Technology
   b Billboards Past and Present
   c How Information Is Sold
   d A New Level of Advertising

2 What does a digital billboard's camera look for?
   a a person's fashion style
   b what a person is carrying
   c a person's age and gender
   d whether someone is alone

3 What is the main idea of the second paragraph?
   a High-tech billboards do not collect personal information.
   b People do not mind the billboards tested in Japan and in the U.S.
   c Advertisers buy information about consumers on the Internet.
   d People are worried about the type of information collected by billboards.

4 Why does the passage mention Google?
   a It is an example of a search engine that sells information to companies.
   b It is better than other search engines in gathering information.
   c It has started using high-tech billboards to get information.
   d It plans to develop better ways to profile Internet users.

5 Because of advertising profiling, a person buying airline tickets online will _____ .
   a see ads for hotels and car rental companies
   b get better prices on their airline tickets
   c see no ads on the airline's website
   d be offered discounts on shoes and clothing

6 In the passage, the writer says that video billboards _____ .
   a allow people on the street to use the Internet
   b show movies and commercials
   c display information about the weather and news
   d are placed inside stores and buildings

7 What is the reason for advertisers making high-tech billboards?
   a People ignore regular advertisements.
   b Regular billboards are not in good locations.
   c It is cheaper to make high-tech billboards.
   d People are suspicious of regular advertising.

SELF CHECK

A Here is a list of all the reading skills in *ACTIVE Skills for Reading Book 2*. For each skill, say whether you found the skill useful, not useful, or you need more work with it. Check (✓) one of the boxes.

Reading skill	Useful	Not useful	I need work
Describing a Process			
Finding Definitions			
Identifying Main and Supporting Ideas			
Identifying Main Ideas within Paragraphs			
Making Inferences			
Noticing Patterns			
Predicting			
Predicting Vocabulary			
Previewing			
Recognizing Facts			
Recognizing Sequence of Events			
Scanning for Details			
Scanning for Numbers			
Scanning for Proper Nouns			
Skimming			
Skimming For General Ideas			
Skimming to Assess a Passage			
Understanding Cause and Effect			
Understanding the Main Ideas			
Using Headings to Understand Main Ideas			

B Here are the four fluency strategies covered in the Review Units. For each strategy, say whether you found it useful, not useful, or if you need more work with it. Check (✔) one of the boxes.

Fluency strategy	Useful	Not useful	I need work
PRO			
PQR+E			
KWL			
Reading ACTIVEly			

C Look again at the *Are You an ACTIVE Reader?* quiz on page 10 and complete the chart again. How has your reading fluency improved since you started this course?

Reading Review 7: The Life of a Food Critic

Fluency Practice

Time yourself as you read through the passage. Try to read as fluently as you can. Record your time in the Reading Rate Chart on page 176. Then answer the questions on the next page.

The Life of a Food Critic

1 You've seen restaurant reviews in newspapers, or perhaps in magazines or on the Internet. People read these reviews when they want to know about the quality and price of the food at a restaurant. Or maybe they're looking for a restaurant with a distinctive atmosphere—dark and romantic, bright and cheerful, or modern and sophisticated. But who writes the articles? Who gets paid to eat? Those
5　lucky people are food critics.

2 Food critics are journalists who eat at restaurants and write reviews that give readers the feeling that they have visited the restaurant themselves. The articles almost always include a description of the restaurant, for example, whether it is nicely decorated or has a beautiful view of the ocean. The menu, prices, and service are generally described as well, but a food critic's main task is to write about their
10　opinion of the food.

3 For "foodies"—people who love and study food and cooking—dining is a feast for the senses, not just for the stomach. Food critics may tell readers about the colors of fresh vegetables, the silky texture of a soup, or the rich aroma of a perfectly cooked chicken. They will mention whether they were listening to soft music while they ate, or the noises of pots and pans being washed in the restaurant's kitchen.
15　And most importantly, they will describe the taste of every dish on the table, starting with the appetizer and ending with the dessert. Every detail of the meal is important.

4 All of this may sound easy enough, but food critics do face some challenges. First, food critics must be excellent writers. Their job is to give accurate information in an entertaining way because newspapers and other publications want the restaurant review to be an enjoyable feature. It is also important for
20　food critics to be very observant by nature, and to have an excellent memory, since taking notes at the table is not something typical customers do.

5 Looking like a typical customer is essential for remaining anonymous, but is perhaps the most difficult challenge. Food critic Ruth Reichl, former editor-in-chief of *Gourmet* magazine, used to go to restaurants wearing disguises so that she received the same food and service as any other diner.

6 25　Despite the challenges, a career as a food critic appeals to many people. Anyone who is thinking about becoming a food critic should start by developing strong writing skills and learning as much about food and cooking as possible.

410 words　　**Time taken** _____

Reading Comprehension

1 Food critics are _____ .
   a restaurant owners
   b professional cooks
   c professional writers
   d magazine editors

2 Which of the following would probably NOT be included in a restaurant review?
   a a description of a restaurant's atmosphere
   b information about a restaurant's hiring procedures
   c information about a restaurant's prices
   d a description of a restaurant's food

3 What is the purpose of paragraph 3?
   a to say that a critic must use all his or her senses when at a restaurant
   b to teach critics what they need to pay attention to when at a restaurant
   c to show that it is a very difficult job being a food critic
   d to say that the taste of the food is the most important detail of a review

4 Why does the author mention soft music and the noises of pots and pans being washed?
   a because food critics must listen carefully to the waiters
   b because it's important for restaurants to use clean dishes
   c because food critics generally focus on the positive
   d because food critics must pay attention to every single detail

5 According to the passage, food critics need a good memory because _____ .
   a they have to avoid taking notes at the table
   b they have very busy schedules every day
   c they like having a challenging job
   d they need to remember which restaurants they have been to

6 Why did Ruth Reichl go to restaurants wearing disguises?
   a She didn't want to get special food and service.
   b She didn't want her friends to know she was a food critic.
   c She enjoyed seeing people's reactions.
   d She had a different job during the day.

7 How does the writer end the passage?
   a with a writing tip
   b with a warning
   c with a personal example
   d with advice

Time yourself as you read through the passage. Try to read as fluently as you can. Record your time in the Reading Rate Chart on page 176. Then answer the questions on the next page.

THE URBAN GARDENER

Cities are home to skyscrapers and apartment buildings, and it's rare to find wide, open spaces within them. With limited space for parks and gardens, architects and city planners often find it challenging to incorporate greenery in neighborhoods. One creative solution is to grow plants on unused areas like walls and rooftops. It's a popular idea, and now rooftop gardens and green walls have been sprouting up[1] in cities around the world.

5   There are many benefits to having green spaces to the urban landscape. Adding gardens to rooftops or walls can create a pleasant environment— what was once a gray cement wall can become a colorful, blooming garden. The CaxiaForum art gallery in Madrid, Spain, is a famous example—one of its walls is covered with 15,000 plants from over 250 different species.
10 In other cities, green walls are being used more functionally, to cover up construction sites and empty buildings and to prominently decorate the lobbies of office buildings.

Using plants to cover walls and rooftops can also keep cities cooler in the summer. Buildings and roads absorb the sun's heat and hold it, causing a
15 building or neighborhood to stay warmer longer. Plants, on the other hand, provide an enormous amount of shade. There is evidence that growing a roof or wall garden can lower a building's energy costs. Many cities offer tax discounts to businesses with these features.

the green wall at
CaxiaForum Madrid

In New York City, public schools plant rooftop gardens that can reduce
20 heating and cooling costs. In addition to saving the school money, teachers and parents love the gardens because of their educational value—it's a fun and healthy way for their kids to investigate the world around them. "For the children, it's exciting when you grow something edible,"[2] said Lauren Fontana, principal of a New York public school.

These green spaces are also used to grow food. In recent years, rooftop gardens have slowly been
25 included in the "local food movement." This is based on the concept that locally grown food reduces pollution since it does not have to be transported far. Vegetables are being grown in rooftop gardens by schools, churches, neighborhoods and even restaurants. Chef Rick Bayless serves "Rooftop Salsa" at his restaurant in Chicago, U.S.A., using only ingredients grown in his rooftop garden.

Rooftop gardens and green walls may require a bit more effort to grow and maintain. However, hard work
30 always brings rewards, and with green spaces, the rewards are plentiful.

[1]When something **sprouts up**, it appears suddenly. A **sprout** is a young plant.
[2]Something that is **edible** can be eaten.

406 words   **Time taken** _____

Unit 2
Chapter 1

accommodation /əkɒməˈdeɪʃən/ *n.* buildings or rooms where people stay, especially in a hotel: *I need to look for accommodation as soon as I move to a new country.*

basic /ˈbeɪsɪk/ *adj.* the simplest and most necessary part of something: *A basic hotel room has a bed and a bathroom, and maybe an air conditioner.*

eager /ˈiɡər/ *adj.* very excited about something that is going to happen soon: *The little girl was eager to ride a plane for the first time.*

exhausting /eɡˈzɔːstɪŋ/ *adj.* very tiring: *I've had an exhausting day, so I'm going to bed.*

fabulous /ˈfæbjələs/ *adj.* great, wonderful: *We had a fabulous time on our vacation!*

possession /pəˈzeʃən/ *n.* a piece of property, a belonging: *Her most valuable possession is a car worth $40,000.*

range /reɪndʒ/ *n.* a number of different things of the same kind: *You can find a range of hair products at a beauty salon.*

unique /juːˈniːk/ *adj.* one of a kind: *Each person in the world has a unique personality.*

_____   _____

_____   _____

Chapter 2

assume /əˈsum/ *v.* to think something is true without proof: *I didn't call because I assumed you were busy.*

authorized /ˈɔːθəˌraɪzd/ *v.* to give official permission for something: *You aren't authorized to be in this area.*

departure /dɪˈpɑːrtʃər/ *n.* a leaving: *My departure for Los Angeles is at 8 a.m. tomorrow.*

expire /ɪkˈspaɪər/ *v.* to end or become unusable after a period of time: *The milk in the refrigerator expires on Tuesday.*

precaution /prɪˈkɔːtʃən/ *n.* a step taken in advance to prevent harm: *She took the precaution of bringing a sweater in case it got cold on the trip.*

purchase /ˈpɜrtʃəs/ *v.* to buy something: *I purchased my first car when I was 17.*

sincere /sɪnˈsiːr/ *adj.* honest in one's thought and action, true: *Her love for you is sincere; she will stay with you in bad times.*

vulnerable /ˈvʌlnərəbəl/ *adj.* describing a person who is easily harmed, hurt, or attacked: *An older person is more vulnerable to sickness.*

_____   _____

_____   _____

Unit 3
Chapter 1

credits /ˈkrɛdɪts/ *n.* a list of people who made a movie, etc.: *The movie star's name was first in the credits.*

crucial /ˈkruʃəl/ *adj.* very important: *It's crucial that children eat a healthy breakfast each morning.*

director /dəˈrɛktər/ *n.* the person who decides how something appears on stage or on screen: *The director of the film was Steven Spielberg.*

exclusive /ɪkˈsklusɪv/ *adv.* only involving the thing(s) mentioned: *This sale is exclusively for members.*

production /prəˈdʌkʃən/ *n.* the making of a movie: *Production on the new movie will start next month.*

scene /siːn/ *n.* one part of a movie: *I cried while watching the last scene of the movie.*

studio /ˈstudioʊ/ *n.* a place where an artist works: *We take lessons at a ballet studio.*

transform /trænsˈfɔrm/ *v.* to change completely: *This book transformed my life; you should read it!*

_____   _____

_____   _____

Chapter 2

ambition /æmˈbɪʃən/ *n.* a strong desire to achieve something: *Lou's ambition was to become a doctor.*

debut /ˈdeɪbyu/ *n.* the first public performance or appearance: *The party was to celebrate the debut of the CD.*

influential /ˌɪnfluˈɛnʃəl/ *adj.* having the power to change people's thinking: *The mayor was very influential in planning the museum.*

inspiration /ˌɪnspəˈreɪʃən/ *n.* getting a good idea of what to do: *My inspiration to paint comes from nature.*

metaphor /ˈmɛtəˌfɔr/ *n.* describes something by referring to it as something else and saying the two things have similar qualities: *The poet used a metaphor to say people are the same as trees.*

passion /ˈpæʃən/ *n.* a very strong feeling or belief: *The singer said her passion for music comes from her mother.*

preserve /prɪˈzɜrv/ *v.* to save something or someone from being harmed or destroyed: *We are using less paper in the office to help preserve the forest.*

represent /ˌriprɪˈzɛnt/ *v.* to be or have the same meaning as something else: *A wedding ring represents the love between two people.*

_____   _____

_____   _____

Unit 4
Chapter 1

achievement /əˈtʃivmənt/ *n.* something important and difficult that is done: *The Nobel Peace Prize is given to people who make great achievements.*

aspire /əˈspaɪər/ *n.* to desire and work toward achieving something: *He has aspired to be in the Olympics since he was a young boy.*

exotic /ɪgˈzɒtɪk/ *adj.* unusual or interesting, usually foreign: *The model has an exotic look.*

feat /fiːt/ *n.* an impressive achievement: *The circus acrobats performed a dangerous feat, walking across a rope high in the air.*

goal /goʊl/ *n.* something you want to do in the future: *The goal of this meeting is to make a decision.*

record /ˈrekɜːrd/ *n.* the best time, distance, etc., in an athletic event: *She holds the world record for the 100-meter dash.*

talent /ˈtælənt/ *n.* being able to do something very well without practice: *Wayne has a great talent for riding horses.*

verify /ˈvɛrəˌfaɪ/ *v.* to say that something is true: *The newspaper verified that the factory was closing.*

_____   _____

_____   _____

Chapter 2

aggressive /əˈgrɛsɪv/ *adj.* acting as if you want to fight or attack someone: *Be careful; this dog is very aggressive and may bite.*

amateur /ˈæməˌtʃʊər/ *n.* someone who is still learning, not a professional: *This class is for amateur photographers.*

coach /koʊtʃ/ *n.* a person who teaches, especially a sports team: *My coach wants me to run two miles before every practice.*

enthusiastic /ɛnˌθuziˈæstɪk/ *adj.* very excited: *I'm not very enthusiastic about doing the dinner dishes.*

professional /prəˈfɛʃənəl/ *adj.* related to a profession (e.g. medicine or law) or a person who makes his or her living as an artist or athlete: *Professional football players must train hard.*

role model /roʊl ˈmɒdl/ *n.* a person who people admire and want to act like: *Michael Jordan was my childhood role model.*

sense of humor /sɛns ʌv ˈhyumər/ *phr.* the ability to understand and laugh at funny things: *Jack got mad at the joke; he has no sense of humor.*

tournament /ˈtʊərnəmənt/ *n.* a competition with a series of games until there is one winner: *The winner of the tournament receives a check for $100,000.*

_____   _____

_____   _____

Unit 5
Chapter 1

breathe /briːθ/ *v.* to take air into your lungs and send it out again: *In the mountains, you can breathe fresh air.*

complex /kəmˈplɛks/ *adj.* difficult, with many parts or pieces: *Economics is a very complex subject.*

consist of /kənˈsɪst ʌv/ *v.* to have or to depend on something: *A team consists of a leader and a few followers.*

illness /ˈɪlnɪs/ *n.* being sick or unwell: *Did the doctor say your illness is serious?*

injury /ˈɪndʒəriː/ *n.* to hurt your body: *A broken arm or leg is a very common injury in extreme sports.*

suffer /ˈsʌfər/ *v.* to have an unpleasant or difficult experience: *Many people suffered through the war.*

surgery /ˈsɜrdʒəriː/ *n.* medical treatment when a doctor cuts open the body to fix or remove something: *My father has a weak heart and needs surgery to make him better.*

treatment /ˈtriːtmənt/ *n.* a method to make something unwell better: *The doctor suggested a few home treatments, such as hot baths.*

_____ _____

_____ _____

Chapter 2

blind /blaɪnd/ *adj.* to not be able to see: *A blind person uses a walking stick when walking down the street alone.*

bounce /baʊns/ *v.* to move away from a surface after hitting it: *The pebble bounced off the surface of the water.*

capable /ˈkeɪpəbəl/ *adj.* having the qualities or abilities needed: *My new washing machine is capable of washing 20 pounds of clothes at one time.*

overcome /ˌoʊvərˈkʌm/ *v.* to control a feeling or problem that was preventing you from doing something: *Only after Rodney overcomes his fear of water will he be able to enjoy swimming.*

phenomenon /fɪˈnɒməˌnɒn/ *n.* an event or situation that cannot be explained: *The northern lights of Alaska and Western Canada is one natural phenomenon I hope to see one day.*

refine /rɪˈfaɪn/ *v.* to make something better by making small changes: *Your plan is almost ready; it only needs to be refined slightly.*

sensitive /ˈsɛnsɪtɪv/ *adj.* reacting easily to very small changes: *I wear sunglasses because my eyes are sensitive to light.*

sight /saɪt/ *n.* the ability to see: *The sight in my right eye is better than in my left eye.*

_____ _____

_____ _____

Unit 6
Chapter 1

decorate /ˈdekəreɪt/ *v.* to beautify, to make festive: *We decorated our house for the holidays.*

display /dɪsˈpleɪ/ *v.* to place in a position to be seen: *The store displays its goods in glass cases.*

precious /ˈpreʃəs/ *adj.* extremely valuable; that should not be wasted: *My time is very precious.*

preserve /prəˈzɜːrv/ *v.* to guard, to protect from harm or change: *The ancient pot was placed in a special room to preserve it.*

define /dɪˈfaɪn/ *v.* to explain something, to give the meaning: *You should define your point before trying to argue it.*

supplies /səˈplaɪz/ *n.* a quantity of goods of a specific kind necessary for an operation: *That farm buys its supplies of feed and grain from the local feed store.*

throw (something) **away** /təˈθrəʊ əˈweɪ/ *v.* to discard, to get rid of: *He threw away the old newspapers.*

universal /yuːnəˈvɜːrsəl/ *adj.* found or practiced everywhere: *Poverty is a universal problem; it happens all over the world.*

_____ _____

_____ _____

Chapter 2

approximately /əˈprɒksəmɪtliː/ *adv.* estimated, about: *My dog weighs approximately ten kilograms.*

convert /kənˈvɜːrt/ *v.* to change from one form to another: *I want to convert the extra bedroom in my apartment to an office.*

detail /ˈdiːteɪl/ *n.* a small point: *There is one detail in the contract that is unclear to me.*

isolated /ˈaɪsəˌleɪtɪd/ *adj.* to make alone or to be far away from others: *When I want to feel isolated, I go to my house in the mountains.*

loyal /ˈlɔɪəl/ adj. following and supporting a friend or organization: *The store gives special discounts to its loyal customers.*

persuade /pɜːrˈsweɪd/ *v.* to lead a person or group to believe or do something by arguing or reasoning with them: *I persuaded my friend to join me on vacation.*

response /rɪˈspɒns/ *n.* a reaction to something done beforehand: *I sent a letter to my brother, but I've yet to get a response.*

switch /swɪtʃ/ *n.* to change quickly and completely: *To lose weight, Bill switched from regular milk to low-fat milk.*

_____ _____

_____ _____

Unit 7
Chapter 1

appealing /əˈpiːlɪŋ/ *adj.* interesting or attractive: *Action movies aren't appealing to me.*

capture /ˈkæptʃər/ *v.* to film or record for the purpose of preserving: *You should capture the moment with a photograph.*

extinct /ɪkˈstɪŋkt/ *adj.* something that has ended or died out: *Many animals are in danger of going extinct.*

format /ˈfɔrmæt/ *n.* the way in which something is presented: *My computer can't play this format of DVD.*

genre /ˈʒɑnrə/ *n.* type or style of music, art, or literature: *The library has books of almost every genre.*

lyrics /ˈlɪrɪks/ *n.* the words of a song: *The lyrics to that song are very meaningful to me.*

roots /ruːts/ *n.* the place or culture that something or someone comes from: *The roots of the problem go back hundreds of years.*

essential /əˈsɛnʃəl/ *adj.* necessary, very important: *Water and air are both essential for human life.*

_____   _____

_____   _____

Chapter 2

album /ˈælbəm/ *n.* a collection of music put on a record or CD: *Have you heard Justin Bieber's new album?*

boundary /ˈbaʊndəriː/ *n.* a real or imaginary line that makes the edge of a location: *China shares a natural boundary with Russia.*

incorporate /ɪnˈkɔrpərɪt/ *v.* to include things into a group: *Modern dance is very different from ballet as it incorporates free movement and loose clothing.*

mature /məˈtʊər/ *adj.* becoming older and wiser: *He is very mature for his age.*

pioneer /ˌpaɪəˈnɪər/ *n.* the first person to do something or to work on something: *Carl Jung was a pioneer in the field of psychology.*

release /riːˈliːs/ *v.* to publish a book, DVD, or CD: *Dr. Phillips' book will be released on Tuesday.*

revolution /ˌrɛvəˈluʃən/ *n.* a complete change in thinking or methods: *Coco Chanel's designs created a revolution in women's fashion.*

statement /ˈsteɪtmənt/ *n.* something written or said that tells an opinion or gives facts: *In his statement, the man said that he was not at home during the robbery.*

_____   _____

_____   _____

Unit 8
Chapter 1

campus /ˈkæmpəs/ *n.* the land and buildings of a university or college: *I like to study at the library on campus.*

concept /ˈkɒnsɛpt/ *n.* an idea about how something is or should be done: *I am good at dreaming up concepts but not very good at applying them!*

enterprising /ˈɛntərˌpraɪzɪŋ/ *adj.* able to make money from new, interesting ideas: *The company was failing until the owner's enterprising son became its leader.*

expand /ɪkˈspænd/ *v.* to get bigger: *The farmer wanted to expand so that he could grow more crops.*

retail /ˈriːteɪl/ *n.* concerning the sale of things to people in stores: *A cash register is the most important piece of equipment in a retail store.*

spur /spɜr/ *v.* motivate, inspire: *The man thanked his grandfather for spurring him on to start his own business.*

stationery /ˈsteɪʃəˌnɛriː/ *n.* products used for writing letters and notes: *I'll use the stationery with my name on it to write the thank-you letter.*

resource /ˈrisɔrs/ *n.* money, skills, or time that is available when needed: *Students who go to schools with a lot of resources are more likely to do well.*

_____   _____

_____   _____

Chapter 2

fundamental /ˌfʌndəˈmɛntl/ *adj.* most important and necessary part of something: *We learn our fundamental values from our parents.*

inclined to /ɪnˈklaɪnd tuː/ *phr. v.* to believe something is likely to be correct: *I'm inclined to believe my brother's story about being late.*

investigate /ɪnˈvɛstɪˌgeɪt/ *v.* to try to find the truth or cause: *After investigating the fire, we think it was caused by a gas leak.*

opinion /əˈpɪnyən/ *n.* a personal belief that is not factual: *Are you asking for my opinion?*

persuasive /pərˈsweɪsɪv/ *adj.* to make other people believe something or do what is asked: *I changed my mind because of your persuasive arguments.*

regulation /ˌrɛgyəˈleɪʃən/ *n.* official rule: *You cannot light fireworks at the park because of the city's regulations.*

theory /ˈθɪəriː/ *n.* an idea that explains why something happens but has not been proven to be true: *Dr. Bell likes to tell his theories to anyone who will listen.*

thrive /θraɪv/ *v.* to do exceptionally well: *Jacob is thriving in his new job.*

_____   _____

_____   _____

Unit 9
Chapter 1

consume /kənˈsuːm/ *v.* to eat and drink: *That big guy consumed six bottles of beer and three hamburgers.*

culinary /ˈkyuləˌnɛri/ *n.* related to food: *The travel agent promised that the vacation would be a culinary adventure.*

cure /kyʊər/ *v.* to fix an illness completely: *There is no cure for the common cold, other than lots of rest and water.*

enhance /ɛnˈhæns/ *v.* to make more attractive or improved: *Scott wears green to enhance the color of his eyes.*

equipment /ɪˈkwɪpmənt/ *n.* the tools and other things needed to do a job or activity: *Bob made a list of equipment he needed to build the bookshelf.*

evolve /ɪˈvɒlv/ *v.* to change for the better: *Do you believe that humans evolved from monkeys?*

extract /ˈɛkstrækt/ *v.* to take out: *Joe extracted the tiny piece of glass stuck in Jenny's finger.*

resemble /rɪˈzɛmbəl/ *v.* to look like: *Rebecca and Dan liked to talk about who their baby resembled more.*

_____   _____

_____   _____

Chapter 2

crave /kreɪv/ *v.* to want something very much: *I crave chocolate after meals.*

decay /dɪˈkeɪ/ *v.* to slowly become destroyed: *You can take vitamins to help your bones stay strong and not decay.*

distinctive /dəˈstɪŋktɪv/ *adj.* different from others, special: *Spices give that dish its distinctive flavor.*

moderation /ˌmɒdəˈreɪʃən/ *n.* in healthy or reasonable amounts: *I like to eat cake, but only in moderation.*

nature /ˈneɪtʃər/ *n.* the basic character or quality of something: *It's not in Jack's nature to share.*

nutritional /nyuˈtrɪʃənəl/ *n.* related to the vitamins, minerals, etc., in food: *Sugar has very little nutritional value.*

stimulate /ˈstɪmyʊˌleɪt/ *v.* to increase energy or activity: *Taking long walks really stimulates my creativity.*

undergo /ˌʌndərˈgəʊ/ *v.* to experience something: *Your doctor will probably tell you not to eat anything before undergoing surgery.*

_____   _____

_____   _____

Unit 10
Chapter 1

access /ˈækses/ *v.* the right to enter a place or use a thing: *You need a password to access the Internet.*

content /ˈkɒntent/ *n.* information: *The company's website looks good but it contains no content.*

ignore /ɪgˈnɔr/ *v.* to not pay attention to something on purpose: *Jill is ignoring Bob's phone calls.*

interactive /ˌɪntərˈæktɪv/ adj. something that a person can communicate with or that responds to a user's actions: *People prefer to have more interactive content today.*

prominently /ˈprɒmənəntli:/ *adv.* in an important way, easily seen: *Her new book is displayed prominently in bookstores.*

subtle /ˈsʌtl/ *adj.* not easy to notice: *My two dogs are both brown, with only a subtle difference in color.*

visible /ˈvɪzəbəl/ *adj.* something that can be seen: *On a clear day, the ocean is visible from my house.*

virtually /ˈvɜrtʃuəli:/ *adv.* almost, practically: *Virtually all libraries have computers people can use for free.*

_____   _____

_____   _____

Chapter 2

consumer /kənˈsumər/ *n.* someone who uses a product: *Businesses use Facebook to find new consumers.*

flatter /ˈflætər/ *v.* to say something to make a product or person look or feel good: *The boy flattered the girl he liked by saying her dress was pretty.*

insensitive /ɪnˈsensɪtɪv/ *adj.* not noticing or caring about another person's feelings: *How can you be so insensitive?*

make fun of *exp.* to say something that hurts or upsets someone: *It was mean to make fun of my sister's height.*

publicity /pʌˈblɪsɪti:/ *n.* news to make a product or event popular: *With good publicity, a product can go from unknown to popular.*

slogan /ˈsloʊgən/ *n.* a saying or phrase that expresses a group's or a company's main message: *"Just do it" is a very well-known slogan.*

submit /səbˈmɪt/ *v.* to give to somebody for their approval: *The application should be submitted before August 5th.*

supply /səˈplaɪ/ *v.* to provide something that is wanted or needed: *The race's organizers supplied water for the runners.*

_____   _____

_____   _____

Unit 11
Chapter 1

alternative /ɔlˈtɜrnətɪv/ *n.* another option: *One alternative to buying a pet in a pet store is adopting one from a shelter.*

anticipate /ænˈtɪsəˌpeɪt/ *v.* to expect something to happen and to be ready for it: *Will you be home tomorrow? I anticipate a few packages arriving in the mail.*

chemical /ˈkɛmɪkəl/ *n.* a substance in chemistry or made from a chemical process: *It is common to clean a bathroom or kitchen with strong chemicals like bleach.*

consequence /ˈkɒnsɪˌkwɛns/ *n.* something that happens as a result of an action: *If you break the law, you might face consequences like going to jail.*

struggle /strʌgəl/ *v.* to deal with something with great difficulty: *She always struggles to finish her food.*

devastating /ˈdɛvəˌsteɪtɪŋ/ *v.* something badly damaging: *An earthquake can have devastating effects on a city.*

keen /kiːn/ *adj.* interested in: *I'm keen to try the new Indian restaurant.*

sustainable /səˈsteɪnəbəl/ *adj.* to be able to continue without causing damage: *The woman moved to the countryside in hopes of living a more sustainable lifestyle.*

_____   _____

_____   _____

Chapter 2

account for /əˈkaʊnt fɔr/ *phr. v.* to form an amount or part of something: *The cafe owner says the sale of coffee drinks accounts for 80 percent of his store's income.*

adopt /əˈdɒpt/ *v.* to start to use a particular style or behavior: *She adopted a British accent while living in London.*

deprive /dɪˈpraɪv/ *v.* to stop something from happening or being used: *Homeless children are deprived of food, but more importantly a peaceful, happy childhood.*

estimated /ˈɛstəˌmeɪtɪd/ *adj.* approximate, about: *I pay an estimated 20 percent in taxes.*

ethical /ˈɛθɪkəl/ *adj.* relating to the idea of what is right and wrong: *It's not ethical for companies to pay their workers so little.*

impact /ˈɪmpækt/ *n.* an effect that is large or important: *No one could have predicted the impact the iPhone would have on communication.*

modify /ˈmɒdəˌfaɪ/ *v.* to change or alter partially: *I have to modify the design slightly for it to work.*

vital /ˈvaɪtl/ *n.* very important or necessary: *At this company we believe every employee is vital to our success.*

_____   _____

_____   _____

Unit 12
Chapter 1

alarming /əˈlɑrmɪŋ/ *adj.* making someone feel worried or scared: *Hearing strange noises in your home at night can be very alarming.*

accumulate /əˈkyumyəˌleɪt/ *v.* to gradually become more and more: *He accumulated enough savings to buy a house.*

ambitious /æmˈbɪʃəs/ *adj.* (of a plan) large-scale, needing a lot of work to succeed: *Jamie Oliver's plan to improve school lunches across the country was very ambitious.*

launch /lɔntʃ/ *v.* to start something big and important: *The magazine launched its first issue with a big party.*

persistence /pərˈsɪstəns/ *n.* determination to do something that is difficult and that other people do not support: *Only with persistence will you be able to find enough money to start your business.*

unite /yuˈnaɪt/ *v.* to come together or form a group to achieve something: *The Internet has helped unite people around the world.*

volunteer /vɔːlənˈtiːr/ *v.* to agree to do something of one's own free will rather than by necessity: *My father volunteers his time at the church.*

waste /weɪst/ *n.* unwanted or worthless materials left after a process: *The factory has to pay money to remove its waste.*

_____   _____

_____   _____

Chapter 2

availability /əˈveɪləˈbɪlitiː/ *n.* being easily found and used: *The availability of ice cream decreases in cold weather.*

drastically /ˈdræstɪk/ *adv.* extreme and sudden: *The new plan is drastically different from the original one.*

endangered /ɛnˈdeɪndʒərd/ *adj.* putting someone or something in danger of being hurt, damaged, or destroyed: *The bald eagle is on the list of endangered animals.*

exceed /ɪkˈsiːd/ *v.* to be more than (what is expected): *Sales of the new product exceeded our estimates.*

lack /læk/ *n.* when there is not enough of something: *Amy lacked the time to do everything she needed to before her trip.*

shortage /ˈʃɔrtɪdʒ/ *n.* a state of not having enough, a lack of something: *A shortage of oil made gasoline more expensive.*

strain /streɪn/ *n.* worry that is caused by working or thinking too much: *Moving many heavy boxes put a strain on Henry's back.*

sustain /səˈsteɪn/ *v.* to be used at a level that won't damage the environment: *The wood for this furniture is taken from a sustainable source.*

_____   _____

_____   _____

Prefixes, Roots and Suffixes

Here is a list of prefixes, roots and suffixes that appear in this book.

Prefixes

a, ad movement to or change into: *advance*, *arrive*, *attend*; **con/com** with or together: *connection*, *communicate*; **cross-** across: *cross-country*, *cross-cultural*; **dis** not, negative: *disappear*, *disapprove*, *disconnect*; **ex** upwards, completely, without, or former: *exhausting*, *experience*, *exclusive*; **im/in** not, negative: *impossible*, *incorrect*, *insecure*; **in** related to inside or inwards: *income*; **inter** between two or more places or groups: *Internet*, *international*; **kilo** a thousand: *kilogram*, *kilometer*; **micro** very small: *microphone*; **milli** related to thousand: *million*, *milliliter*, *millimeter*; **mis** badly or wrongly: *miserable*; **over** more: *overestimate*, *overpay*; **pre** done before or in advance: *precaution*, *predict*, *prepaid*; **re** again or back: *return*, *recycle*, *renew*; **sub** below or under: *submit*; **tele** far: *television*, *telephone*; **trans** across: *transportation*, *transform*; **un** not, negative: *unaware*, *unethical*, *unidentified*, *unthinkable*; **under** less: *underway*, *underweight*; **uni** one: *university*, *united*; **up** higher or improved: *uphill*, *upgrade*, *update*; **well-** done well or a lot: *well-known*, *well-liked*

Root Words

bio related to life: *biology*, *biography*; **geo** related to the earth: *geographic*, *geology*; **phon** related to the sound: *phonics*; **physio** nature/body: *physiology*; **psych** related to the mind: *psychologist*; **pub** related to people: *publicity*, *public*; **socio** related to the culture: *sociology*; **vit/viv** life: *vitamin*, *vivid*

Suffixes

able full of: *beatable*, *believable*; **al** used to make an adjective from a noun: *additional*, *personal*, *national*, *vital*; **an/ian** relating to: *American*, *Australian*, *Italian*; **ant/ent** indicating an adjective: *important*, *independent*; **ate** used to make a verb from a noun: *decorate*, *originate*; **ation/ution/ition** used to make a noun from a verb: *combination*, *resolution*, *competition*; **dom** state of being: *freedom*, *kingdom*; **eer** one who does something: *pioneer*, *volunteer*; **en** used to form verbs meaning to increase a quality: *harden*, *threaten*, *frighten*; **ence** added to some adjectives to make a noun: *confidence*, *excellence*; **ent** used to make an adjective from a verb: *confident*, *excellent*; **ent** one who does something: *parent*, *student*; **er/or** someone or something that does something: *advertiser*, *competitor*, *reporter*; **er** (after an adjective) more: *faster*, *safer*; **est** (after an adjective) most, ever, any: *safest*; **ful** filled with: *careful*, *powerful*; **hood** state of: *childhood*, *neighborhood*; **ion/sion/tion** indicating a noun: *admiration*, *competition*; **ic** used to make an adjective: *realistic*, *simplistic*; **ine** indicating a verb: *combine*; **ish** relating to: *English*, *distinguish*, *Jewish*; **ist** one who does something: *artist*, *psychologist*, *tourist*; **ity** used to make a noun from an adjective: *charity*, *identity*; **ive** indicating an adjective: *aggressive*, *negative*; **ize/ise** to make or cause to become: *memorize*, *surprise*; **less** without, not having: *hopeless*, *restless*; **logy/ology** the study of: *geology*, *psychology*; **ly** used to form an adverb from an adjective: *especially*, *quickly*; **mate** companion: *roommate*, *classmate*; **ment** used to make a noun from a verb: *improvement*, *measurement*, *government*; **ness** used to make a noun from an adjective: *awareness*, *business*, *friendliness*; **ous/ious** to have or to be full of: *adventurous*, *curious*, *dangerous*; **some** full of: *awesome*, *handsome*; **th** indicating an order: *eighteenth*, *sixth*; **ure** indicating some nouns: *culture*, *temperature*, *candidature*; **y** indicating an adjective: *flashy*, *healthy*

Reading Rate Chart

Use this graph to record your progress for each of the eight Review Reading passages. Find the intersection of your reading rate and your comprehension score. Write the number of the review reading on the chart. Your goal is to place in Quadrant 4.

335	**Quadrant 2**				**Quadrant 4**
320					
305					
290					
275					
260					
245					
230					
215					
200					
185					
170					
155					
140					
125					
110					
95					
80					
65					
50	**Quadrant 1**				**Quadrant 3**
	1 (20%)	2 (40%)	3 (60%)	4 (80%)	5 (100%)

Calculating your words-per-minute (wpm) At the end of each passage you see the number of words in the text (i.e. Practice Reading #1 = 175 words). Divide your time into the number of words in the passage to get your wpm. For example, if you read Practice Reading #1 in 45 seconds, your wpm equals 233 wpm (175/.75 = 233).

Quadrant 1: You are reading slower than 200 wpm with less than 70% comprehension.
Quadrant 2: You are reading faster than 200 wpm with less than 70% comprehension.
Quadrant 3: You are reading slower than 200 wpm with greater than 70% comprehension.
Quadrant 4: You are reading faster than 200 wpm with greater than 70% comprehension.